PRAISE FOR *BAD MEDICINE*

Bad Medicine *is an insider's look at the failure of the justice system in its dealings with Aboriginal lawbreakers. Alberta Provincial Court Judge John Reilly spares no one, including himself, in his belief that a different and non-racist approach would serve First Nations more effectively. He makes a compelling case for "good" medicine to replace the "bad." A must read for anyone connected with Canada's legal system.*

—Catherine Ford,
Author of *Against the Grain: An Irreverent View of Alberta*

Judge John Reilly demonstrates an uncommon understanding of the complex issues and problems confronting Canada's Aboriginal peoples. Were everyone in Canada to share his perspectives we would be much further ahead in overcoming these challenges.

—The Honourable Patrick Brazeau, Senator and former National Chief of the Congress of Aboriginal Peoples

MEDIA COMMENTARY ON JUDGE JOHN REILLY

[John Reilly's] crusade has touched off a nationwide debate about government policies that are designed to foster native self-determination but may condemn another generation of Indians to lives of dependency and despair.

—Steven Pearlstein, *The Washington Post*

Judge John Reilly wanted to expose wrongdoing on the Stoney reserve. What he didn't realize was that powerful forces – in Ottawa, in Edmonton, and in the band itself – had a vested interest in ignoring the problem.

—Gordon Laird, *Saturday Night*

MORE MEDIA COMMENTARY ON JUDGE JOHN REILLY

... here's a judge willing to speak out and actively engineer alternatives and swim bravely against powerful societal currents.

—Bill Kaufmann, *Calgary Sun*

... government dollars flow in and many reserves get huge oil and gas revenues, but housing is pitiful, in some cases water is unclean, and social problems, unemployment and crime are all high. Why is this? Reilly had the courage to ask. He's not alone.

—Linda Slobodian, *Calgary Sun*

Judge Reilly's order was a brave and crazy political stunt. There is little chance that his order will hold up on appeal, but that's not the point. This man, this powerful white man who makes his living moving people from the scenic ghettos we quaintly call "reservations" to the even worse environment of prison, tried to do the right thing.

—Nick Devlin, *FFWD*

At first it appeared little would come of Provincial Court Judge John Reilly's order for an investigation into physical and political squalor on the Stoney Indian reserve, 30 miles west of Calgary.... But now it seems Judge Reilly's intervention has unleashed a maelstrom of activity: in the courts, in Ottawa – and especially in band offices, where frustrated Indians are taking matters into their own hands.

—*Alberta Report*

BAD MEDICINE

*A Judge's Struggle for Justice in a
First Nations Community*

by John Reilly

RMB

Victoria Vancouver Calgary

Rocky Mountain Books
www.rmbooks.com

Library and Archives Canada Cataloguing in Publication

Reilly, John, 1946-
    Bad medicine / John Reilly.

Includes bibliographical references and index.
Issued also in electronic format.
ISBN 978-1-926855-03-5

    1. Reilly, John, 1946-. 2. Judges—Alberta—Biography.
3. Indian reservations—Alberta—Morley. 4. Assiniboine
Indians—Legal status, laws, etc.—Alberta—Morley.
5. Social justice. I. Title.

KE416.R45A3 2010   340.092   C2010-902811-2
KF345.Z9R45 2010

Front cover: adapted from a painting by Stoney artist Roland Rollinmud

Printed in Canada

Rocky Mountain Books acknowledges the financial support for its publishing program from the Government of Canada through the Canada Book Fund (CBF), Canada Council for the Arts, and the province of British Columbia through the British Columbia Arts Council and the Book Publishing Tax Credit.

The interior pages of this book have been produced on 100% post-consumer recycled paper, processed chlorine free and printed with vegetable-based inks.

CONTENTS

To Laura

❖

170°
160°
150°
140°
130°
120°
110°
100°
Russia
Chukchi Bay
Arctic Ocean
Queen Elizabeth
Prince Patrick Island
Beaufort Sea
Parry Islands
Melville Island
Banks Island
Parry Cha
Amundsen Gulf
Prince of Wales Island
Victoria Island
King William Island
Yukon
Koyukuk
Porcupine
60°
Yukon Territory
Great Bear Lake
Whitehorse
Gulf of Alaska
Northwest Territories
Nunavu
Yellowknife
Great Slave Lake
Liard
British Columbia
Canada
Peace
Lake Athabasca
Manitoba
Alberta
Saskatchewan
Queen Charlotte Islands
Reindeer Lake
Churchill
50°
Edmonton
Cedar Lake
Vancouver
Cochrane
Morley
Calgary
Saskatoon
Lake Winnipeg
Pacific Ocean
Victoria
Regina
Lake Manitoba
Winnipeg
Lake of the Woods
Columbia
Missouri
Yellowstone
40°
United States
Great Salt Lake
120°
110°
100°

ACKNOWLEDGEMENTS

In the production of the book:

The Georgetown Research Institute, especially Bob Sandford, and Paul Carrick, who prodded me into writing. My publisher, Don Gorman, who suggested the title and gave me soft deadlines. Joe Wilderson, who made great improvements in the text and made it seem like I was doing it all myself. My sons, Sean and Jamie, and my daughters, Tara and Carlyn, for their prodding and encouragement.

Everyone else who encouraged me to write: Warren and Mary Anna Harbeck, Professor Tony Hall, Nomi Whalen, Stephanie Jardine, Jacqueline Kay and Ruth Gorman (RIP).

In surviving the conflict:

Laura, my warrior bride, who wouldn't let me give up.

My lawyer, Alan Hunter, QC, who devoted his considerable legal talent to my many legal battles and became a friend and mentor in the process (may his soul Rest in Peace), his wife, Ginnie, who kept us fed and cheerful as we worked at it.

The members of the Stoney Nation who taught me about life and relationship and encouraged me to believe I was making a difference: Tina Fox, Marjorie Powderface, Bert Wildman (RIP), Lazarus and Lilly Wesley (RIP), Greg Twoyoungmen, John Robinson and Pauline Twoyoungmen, Wilfred Fox, Aaron and Angela Young, Roland Rollinmud, and Ernest and Belva Wesley.

Members of the media who informed the public of the plight of Aboriginal people and supported my view that the first step in solving the problem is to acknowledge it. Kim Lunman, Bob

Beaty, Mark Lowey, Kevin Martin, Linda Slobodian, Vicki Megrath, Lisa Dempster, Sherri Zickefoose, Camie Leard, Jeff Adams, David Heyman, Monte Stewart, Suzanne Wilton, Nick Devlin, Monica Andreeff, Steve Chase, David Burke, Daffyd Roderick, Mario Toneguzzi, Sheldon Alberts, Bill Kaufmann, Sean Gordon, Catherine Ford, Dale Eisler, Kyra Hoggan, Ben Smales, David Bercuson, Barry Cooper, Steve Pearlstein, Jack Tennant and Peter Cheney.

Others who gave me support and encouragement:

Rose Auger (RIP), John Chief Moon, Dale Auger (RIP), Hansen Twoyoungmen (RIP), Harley and Lois Frank, Garth Pritchard, Jeff and Aileen Williams, Mary Stacey and Jeffrey Perkins.

The judges and court staff who helped me feel a little less like an outsider in the judicial system:

Judge David Tilley (RIP), Judge Pierre Dubé (RIP), Judge Bert Oliver (RIP), Judge Albert Ludwig, Judge Herb Allard, Judge Doug McDonald, Judge Manfred DeLong, Judge Tony Demong (RIP), Judges Don Fraser and Judy Little of Kenora, Ontario, Justice Robert Reilly, Ontario High Court, Judge Syd Wood, Clare Jarman, Keith Kloster (RIP), Sandra Furlonger, Aleya Trott, Jenny Wood, Joyce Sudsbury, Laureen Allary, Roselyn Balanquit-Bernardo, and last but certainly not least, the current Chief Judge of the Provincial Court of Alberta, the Honourable Gail Vickery.

As I was living through the events described in this book, I often felt very alone. As I wrote this page, I realized I had a lot of support and I am grateful to all of those I have mentioned and apologize to those I have missed.

INTRODUCTION

As the judge who had the primary jurisdiction over the Stoney Indian reserve at Morley, Alberta, in the Rocky Mountain foothills just west of Calgary, I became aware of the frightening dysfunction that plagues this reserve and is often typical of reserves across Canada. I resolved to do everything in my power to help these people. My efforts drew me into unexpected conflict, but my conflict was much less of a struggle than what Aboriginal people face every day.

When my chief judge ordered me to leave Canmore because in his opinion I had lost my objectivity with Aboriginal offenders, I became discouraged and just wanted to give in. My wife, Laura, said to me, "You started this fight to help the Stoneys. Are you just going to turn your back on them?"

Another day, when she and I were discussing the possibility of being forced out of our home, she said to me, "You know, we are really lucky." Tired of the struggle, I asked her what she meant.

She said, "We chose this fight. The Stoneys are born into it. They don't get a choice."

In the spring of 1996 I had made a promise to make my court accessible, understandable and effective for the Stoney people. In order to do so, I tried to learn as much as I could about them. My thought was that if I could explain our legal system to them in terms they would understand, they would embrace it and they would see that, even though the system sends people to prison, it is really about protecting people from being punished wrongfully.

What I learned about the Stoneys, but mostly what I learned

from them, changed my life forever. My life became much harder but much better. Harder because my thinking about justice, punishment, relationships and life in general changed, and this put me in conflict with many of my colleagues. I had been the Joe Clark of the Alberta judicial system. I had learned the law and applied it without question. I got along with everyone. I was appointed a judge at 30 years of age because, like Joe Clark, I hadn't offended anyone. But after 20 years on the bench, I was getting to know a whole community of people who seemed to view my glorious justice system as an instrument of their oppression, and I was inclined to agree with them.

Everyone who speaks about the difficulties faced by Native communities seems to have some trite explanation of these difficulties: residential schools, the reserve system, Indian Act government, broken treaties, policies of assimilation. Everyone also seems to have some trite solution: repeal the Indian Act, divide the reserves and issue private land titles, stop giving *them* handouts, educate *them*, assimilate *them*. It's more than a little ironic that some of the suggested solutions are largely what caused the problems in the first place.

My own trite explanation of the problems is: *bad medicine*. My trite solution is: *good medicine*.

I want to tell my story about my experience with the Stoneys because I think that if everyone were to learn the lessons I have learned, some might change their attitude toward the Indian people. We used to say about "handicapped" people, before that term became politically incorrect, that their worst handicap was our attitude toward them. This is certainly true about Indians, Aboriginals, Natives, First Nations, whatever we call them or whatever they call themselves.

My efforts brought me a considerable degree of notoriety. On June 26, 1997, I ordered an investigation of political corruption and financial mismanagement on the reserve. One of the most gratifying aspects of this notoriety was a full-page story about my exploits, in *The Washington Post*, the paper that was credited with bringing down US President Richard Nixon. The writer of that article, Steve Pearlstein, told me that the thing I did, which brought me so much notoriety, was that I broke the taboo that says you do not criticize an Indian chief.

The one I criticized wasn't just any Indian chief. The Reverend Doctor Chief John Snow had the distinction of being an ordained minister of the United Church, a holder of two honorary doctorates, and one of the most noted chiefs in Canada. He was elected chief of the Wesley band of the Stoney tribe (again, the terms used at the time) in 1959 and was re-elected continually for 28 years. In 1992 he lost to Ernest Wesley, but then was re-elected in 1996. In 2000 Snow again lost to Wesley and he finally retired.

For many he was an icon of Aboriginal success and an example of what Aboriginal people are able to accomplish. But I believe his public image was and is a fraud, one of many he committed against his people. To allow this fraud to continue without correction is to allow the abuse the system inflicts on the poorer members of Canadian First Nations to continue.

In November of 2008 Greg Twoyoungmen complained about the University of Calgary accepting a scholarship in the name of the late Reverend Doctor Chief John Snow. The *Cochrane Eagle* did a story about this and I was asked for my opinion. I said: "In my view it calls the integrity of the university into question when they will grant a scholarship in the name of the man who was the antithesis of education on his reserve."

In a subsequent meeting, Chief Judge Gail Vickery informed me that she had received a complaint about me, and showed me a letter from the firm of Wilson Laycraft, Barristers & Solicitors, written by Kenneth E. Staroszik, which stated:

I have been retained by the family and estate of the late John Snow Sr., former chief of the Stoney Wesley First Nation. Chief Snow was also an ordained minister of the United Church of Canada, and a recipient of an honorary doctorate from the University of Calgary.

Chief Snow passed away on June 16, 2006. His funeral was held at the Goodstoney Centre at Morley and was attended by more than 1,000 people. The cover page of the Cochrane Eagle on June 21, 2006, and the accompanying article regarding his funeral are enclosed.

In November 2008 the Cochrane Eagle published an article titled "Award in Snow's Name Hammered by Critics." The article concerns scholarships at the University of Calgary which are in the name of Reverend Dr. Chief Snow. The said article quotes Judge Riley [sic] as follows:

> Reilly said he will likely write a letter of protest to the university. "I'm concerned about the integrity of a university that would have an award in the name of a man who has shown complete disregard for education on the Stoney Indian Reserve," he said. "The most heinous example is that when he returned to office in 1996 he cut out all the adult education programs that were established while he was not in office. This man is the antithesis of education for his people."

Our clients are offended by the judge's comments about their late father. Judge Riley's comments were not made in a judicial proceeding but to a reporter outside the courtroom. Judge Riley knew, or ought to have known, that his comments would be published. Judge Riley knew that Chief John Snow was not alive to defend himself.

Our clients believe that Judge Riley's conduct in giving an

interview to a reporter and in making disparaging comments about Chief Snow is conduct unfitting a sitting judge.

Please consider this letter a formal complaint about Judge Riley's conduct pursuant to section 9.4 of the Provincial Court Act and Part 6 of the Judicature Act.

Yours truly.
WILSON LAYCRAFT
Kenneth E. Staroszik, QC

Chief Judge Vickery was very pleasant about the matter, but indicated that it was a complaint and she would have to respond. She asked if she could say that I regretted the comments I had made. I really wanted to co-operate with Judge Vickery. Working with her was such a pleasant change from her predecessors, with whom I had engaged in years of conflict, but I laughed and said "No." I suggested she could tell Mr. Staroszik that she regretted my comments but I stand behind them, and as a matter of fact I'm writing a book about them. I also suggested that if she were talking to him she might tell him he could at least spell my name correctly.

In my view, the letter was an example of the intimidation used by First Nations elites to hide the truth. I told Greg Twoyoungmen about the letter and the statement that there were a thousand people at the funeral. Greg's comment was: "Yeah, there were a thousand people at the funeral – a few of them came to mourn, the rest came to make sure he was dead."

When I was working on the judgment in the case of *R. v. Hunter*, I sent a draft to Allan Cawsey, who had been the chairman of the Task Force on the Canadian Criminal Justice System and Its Impact on the Indian and Métis People of Alberta. The draft contained criticisms of the tribal government and John Snow. Cawsey's words to me were: "There is no doubt that one of the worst aspects of life on reserves is corrupt tribal governments, but we can't say anything about it."

I have great respect for Allan Cawsey, and gratitude for his role in my appointment as a judge, but I told him I could not accept his admonition not to say anything about corrupt Aboriginal governments. In my view, the then-new provision of the Criminal Code which referred to "circumstances of Aboriginal offenders" required me to consider all the aspects of reserve life as they related to criminal activity, and I believe corrupt tribal governments are a contributing factor.

I have a problem with truth. I have never learned which part of it I am allowed to speak and which part I am not. So here is my story.

❖ I ❖

MY FATHER'S DRUM

If a man does not keep pace with his companions, perhaps it
is because he hears a different drummer. Let him step to the
music which he hears, however measured or far away.
—HENRY DAVID THOREAU,
Walden (1854)

One day as I was driving past Mount Yamnuska, a.k.a. John Laurie Mountain, I thought to myself: "I have stepped to the beat of my father's drum."

The mountain made me think of my father because he and John Laurie were lifelong friends. They had met at Western Canada College, where they were both teachers for a few years in the 1920s.

Laurie was an important figure in the history of both the province and the Stoney people. He founded the Indian Association of Alberta and it was through his efforts that sections in the Indian Act and the Elections Act were amended to allow Indians to vote in federal elections without giving up their treaty rights.

I don't remember ever meeting Laurie, but he would have been a frequent visitor to our family home when I was a child. I look on his friendship with my father as my spiritual connection to the Stoney people. My father would often speak of him and he often mentioned that Laurie was buried on the Stoney reserve. I remember the first time I visited Laurie's grave as being a powerful spiritual experience, but I will speak of that later.

My father was 56 years old the year I was born. People would often assume he was my grandfather. I believe he was the best father ever, and that I benefited hugely from the wisdom and virtue he had attained through a long life well lived.

The experience of growing up with an elderly father may have contributed to my appreciation of the Aboriginal tradition of reverence for their elders, and in any event I now feel tremendously honoured to be able to count among my close friends a number of the Stoney elders.

I have driven past that mountain over a thousand times. My work as the resident Provincial Court judge in Canmore, Alberta, has taken me to the neighbouring town of Cochrane almost every Tuesday and Thursday for 15 years. The route takes me east on the Trans-Canada Highway, across the Bow River, past the Three Sisters (the signature mountain of Canmore), across Dead Man's Flats, around Lac des Arcs and up the hill through the rock cut, from which there is an open view of the flat-sided mountain called Yamnuska.

For those unfamiliar with the history and geography of Alberta, Calgary is one of the most vibrant cities in Canada. When I was born, in the 1940s, the city had a population of about 100,000. Now it numbers more than a million. When I was growing up we proudly called it "Cowtown," as its main claim to fame was the annual rodeo, the Calgary Exhibition & Stampede, "the Greatest Outdoor Show on Earth." The 1970s saw an oil boom in Alberta, and Calgary became the centre of it. Skyscrapers shot up like dandelions and the population mushroomed too.

The original Fort Calgary was at the confluence of the Bow and the Elbow rivers about 100 kilometres east of the Rocky Mountains. For many years the city was contained on the flat lands between the rivers and surrounding hills. Now the cannibalistic urban sprawl goes for miles in every direction.

Many of the buildings and homes in Calgary have glorious views of the Rockies such a short distance to the west, and Canmore, where I live, is just a little way inside the protection of the easternmost slopes and just outside the gates of Banff National Park.

Canmore was originally established as a coalmining town when the railway came through in 1883. The last mine closed in 1979 and the town sat relatively dormant until the Winter Olympics of 1988. The Nordic skiing events were held at Canmore, and the world saw this beautiful place on television. People started coming here, and the town boomed from a population of about 3,000 to eventually more than 15,000.

The Stoney Indian reserve covers about 400 square kilometres of the foothills east of Canmore and west of Calgary. Its western boundary is the Kananaskis River, and it is an irregular-shaped area lying on both sides of the Bow. The reserve stretches along either side of the Trans-Canada Highway to the top of the Scott Lake Hill on the north side of the highway and all the way to the western edge of the town of Cochrane on the south side of the Bow.

Cochrane is a town that will always be special to me. It is struggling with rapid population growth and huge expansion but doing a good job of preserving its western flavour and heritage. Many of the buildings on main street have the squared-off false fronts typical of western-movie sets, and warm days in the summer will see dozens of people enjoying one of the hundred different flavours of ice cream from the storied MacKay's.

The Provincial Building on Main Street (1st St.) is a two-storey red-brick structure that has had a number of different services on the main floor, a former Alberta government liquor store (from the days before liquor was sold by private businesses), an Alberta Treasury Branch bank, education facilities and a health clinic.

The second floor has housed the Provincial Court of Alberta for as long as the building has been there.

In my 35 years as a judge, I have sat in that courtroom more than any other, and it is in that courtroom that all charges laid on the Stoney Indian reserve at Morley are heard.

The Stoney are Nakoda Sioux. Their ancestors migrated from their original territory in what is now North and South Dakota during the smallpox epidemic which decimated their population in the 1500s. They went north through Lake of the Woods and then west across the northern regions of what are now the Canadian prairie provinces and settled along the eastern slopes of the Rocky Mountains.

In their traditional lifestyle they lived in small family groups and moved about the area as nomads. A significant difference between them and the people of the Blackfoot Confederacy was that they hunted mostly deer. Since deer are not large animals, they can be hunted by small groups and they only provide food for a few people. For this reason the Stoney lived in these small, independent groups and only gathered together for sun dances and round dances a few times a year.

The Blackfoot, by comparison, were primarily buffalo hunters, and since buffalo are huge animals that travelled in enormous herds, it would take large groups of people to organize the hunt. When the hunt was successful it would feed great numbers. As a result of this the Blackfoot lived in much larger groups and developed a more complex social system with more recognizable leaders. The Europeans called these leaders "chiefs," and of course that involved their own understanding of what a chief was.

Given the hierarchical and authoritarian culture of Europe, these newcomers to Turtle Island assumed that chiefs were the top of a hierarchy and had authority over their people. The understanding I have of the Native culture generally is that the leaders were much different from what the Europeans thought. There were leaders who were followed for their wisdom and their abilities, but they did not govern by exercising a European-like authority. They were not people to be "obeyed."

In 1877, when First Nations gathered at Blackfoot Crossing, on the Bow River near present-day Cluny, Alberta, to negotiate Treaty 7, Crowfoot of the Siksika and Red Crow of the Kainai would have stood out as leaders because of the large number of followers they had. The Stoney would not have had such distinctive leaders, because they did not share the same lifestyle.

By the time of the treaty talks, the Reverend George McDougall had established his Stoney Mission at Morleyville, and he brought representatives of the Stoney clans with him to Blackfoot Crossing. My impression of what happened is that he would have chosen a number of Stoneys who would have been designated to put their marks on the treaty.

I also understand, and I believe it is a recorded fact, that no one at the signing of Treaty 7 spoke both Stoney and English. The Stoney speak Nakoda Sioux, which, along with Dakota and Lakota, are the three dialects of the Siouan language. During their migration to the eastern slopes, the Stoney, who now call themselves the Stoney Nakoda, had intermingled with the Cree, and there were probably a number of Stoney who spoke Cree and a number of Cree who spoke Stoney, or Nakoda Sioux. Thus the Stoneys' understanding of the document they marked would have depended on their knowledge of Cree and whatever translation was made into Cree. This understanding may have been very rudimentary, since there were no Cree signatories to Treaty 7.

The territory of the Stoney Nakoda First Nation is still shown on maps as the "Stoney Indian Reserve" even though the term "Indian" has become politically incorrect. Yamnuska is a Stoney word meaning "flat-sided mountain."

On this particular day, in August 2000, I had an outstanding matter in the Alberta Court of Appeal, to wit: *The Honourable John Reilly, Judge of the Provincial Court of Alberta v. The Chief Judge of the Provincial Court of Alberta*. I was also scheduled to appear before a judicial inquiry board in the matter of a *Complaint under s. 6.1 of the* Judicature Act *against the Honourable Judge John D. Reilly of the Provincial Court of Alberta.*

Still, it was a beautiful morning. The sun was shining on the face of the mountain, and I was trying hard to shake the nagging anxiety that was ruining my day. This anxiety had become a permanent feature of my life for several years, and I was reflecting on how it all had happened. I had become a judge because I wanted to avoid conflict. I did not like the adversarial nature of the practice of law. When the Judicial Council interviewed me prior to my appointment, I told them I wanted to be a judge because I thought I would be a better referee than a player. That was how it began, and now I was the main player in a matter that had attracted national and international attention. I was in conflict with the chief judge of my court, the chiefs of the Indian reserve I had tried to help, and the chief legal officer of the province of Alberta, the Minister of Justice.

I had been appointed a judge on June 21, 1977. June 21 is National Aboriginal Day. Lieutenant-Governor Ralph Steinhauer signed my appointment. He was Alberta's first Native Lieutenant-Governor and he was born at Morley.

My father was very spiritual and well read. He had many words of wisdom. One oft-repeated comment was: "God takes a hand in these things more than we know." I believe he was right. He would often quote the Protestant hymn by David Bliss called "Dare to be a Daniel; dare to stand alone." As a young man I had hated hearing it. Now, whenever I feel backed against a wall, I like to sing it to myself:

Dare to be a Daniel
Dare to stand alone
Dare to have a purpose firm
Dare to make it known

That day, in my middle age, as I drove past John Laurie Mountain, I realized I had followed that advice. I felt very alone. Only a few of my fellow judges supported me. Judges generally are very conservative. They tend to disapprove of non-traditional action, and my efforts to improve the delivery of justice to the Stoneys had been non-traditional to say the least.

The years and the conflict have changed my thinking about many things: about my country, my history, the criminal justice system and the judiciary. I believe my experience has made me a better person and a better judge, and this is the understanding I seek to share.

❖ 2 ❖

MY CIRCUMSTANCES

Reggie Crowshoe, the cultural guru of the Piikani Nation of the Blackfoot Confederacy, says that when you tell a story you should tell something about yourself. People should know something about the storyteller. So I will engage in a bit of navel-gazing for those who are interested. If I uncover a few of the skeletons in my own family closet, I apologize to those who may be offended. I write this for the benefit of the Stoney people, many of whom suffer from family dysfunction, and it is only fair that I admit to some dysfunction of my own. In any event, it's part of my story.

When I was born there on June 26, 1946, Calgary was a small city where people complained about Eastern dominance and the Crow Rate. (The Crow Rate was the rate charged for shipping grain from anywhere east of the Crowsnest Pass and it was higher than the rate for shipping manufactured goods westward, which put a disproportionate burden on the West.) The "City on the Bow" was fairly compact in size and layout and the outlying towns of Bowness and Forest Lawn were separate entities. The hamlet of Midnapore was a ten-minute drive south from the city limits. Now that trip can take up to an hour, depending on Macleod Trail traffic.

My father was a schoolteacher, born in Sherbrooke, Quebec, in 1890. His uncle, James Reilly, had come west before 1883, before the railway was completed, and served as mayor of Calgary for two terms in the 1890s. His mother, Phoebe (née Broderick) had a sister, Mary Anne, who married Jean-Baptiste-Moïse St-Laurent (my father's Uncle Moses). Their son, Louis, was Prime Minister of Canada from 1948 to 1957.

In 1900 the family moved to Calgary. My father had been sent to a boarding school in South Bend, Indiana, now called the University of Notre Dame. He spent two years there, away from his family and in the care of the Christian Brothers of Ireland. By the time he arrived in Calgary in 1902 his father had completed construction of the house at 337 15th Avenue SW, where I spent my childhood.

My grandfather died in that house in 1910, just ten days after the death of his brother, James. Uncle James had become quite wealthy, and my grandfather had expected to inherit his estate. James died in Victoria, and the will was read in Calgary ten days later. The bulk of the estate was left to my father's brother, Clifford. My grandfather went to the third floor of the house in such a rage that he died there. As a child, I was always afraid to go to that part of the house. It gave me an eerie feeling. My sister agrees with me. There was something up there, whether it was his ghost or the vibrations still reverberating from his anger or just our imaginations fuelled by the story.

It must have been devastating for my father. There was a barn behind the house where he kept a saddle horse (still the main method of transportation in those days). He told me that when his father died he went out to the barn and buried his face in the horse's mane and wept. He said he was closer to his uncle than his father, but losing his father too, just ten days later, was a loss that was almost more than he could bear. He was only 19.

My son, Jamie (named for his great-great-uncle James), is just 15. It is interesting to imagine my father at that age. Uncle James had built and operated the Royal Hotel at the corner of Centre Street and 9th Avenue. The famous lawyer Paddy Nolan stayed there when he first arrived in Calgary. The Catholic missionary

Albert Lacombe also stayed there. At 15 my father was employed running the taxi service, a horse-drawn buggy in which he would chauffeur hotel guests. One of his frequent "fares" was Father Lacombe.

Uncle James had wanted to be the first Lieutenant-Governor of Alberta when it was made a province in 1905. Father Lacombe had significant influence with the federal government of the day, and James had asked him to introduce him to officials who were here to select the person who would fill the position. Lacombe made the introduction but introduced my great-uncle as "the man who runs the hotel," a comment Uncle James was sure destroyed his chance of getting the appointment.

My father attended school at Western Canada College. He went on to the University of Alberta and was in his last year when the First World War began. He told me he hadn't intended to enlist, but that a friend who was on his way to sign up offered to put his name down too. Dad casually said he could, and he did. So Dad was enlisted. He went overseas in 1914 and spent the war in the trenches in Belgium and France. He was wounded by shrapnel close to the end of the war and was not discharged from the army until he was discharged from the military hospital in 1919.

The shrapnel shattered the bones in his right leg and the leg healed shorter than the left, requiring him to wear a built-up shoe for the rest of his life. It would often cause him severe pain. Evidently pieces of shrapnel left in the body will oxidize for years after the external wound has healed. This would happen and he would suffer from it. I was born almost 30 years after that war, and I can remember Dad going to bed in the middle of the day. My mother would tell me it was because his leg was bothering him. Dad wouldn't say so. He never complained. Another of his adages was "Never rehearse the symptoms of dis-ease." He wouldn't allow himself to talk about things that were upsetting him (dis-ease).

"Be careful of the power of suggestion," he'd say. He believed that words create what they say. "You don't look very well" will make a person feel unwell; "You look great!" will make a person feel better.

"Sufficient unto the day is the evil thereof," he would quote. This was a difficult one for me because the syntax was so unusual. It would be easier to understand "The evil of today is sufficient for today" or "For today, today's troubles are enough." Dad would never allow himself to worry about the future.

After my great-uncle James died in 1910, Uncle Clifford, with his newly acquired fortune, purchased the house on the corner of 7th Street and 15th Avenue SW for his mother. That house is now an historic site because the famous women's rights activist Nellie McClung lived there for a number of years. My grandmother lived there until she died in 1920. Dad told me that the last time _____ her was the night before she died. She was on her way up _____ ing she said to him was "Don't worry." He _____ ic for her to say this. She had worried all _____ have been a pretty amazing woman, though. _____ ndfather, I believe was an alcoholic, and yet _____ e four of her five sons complete university. _____ e Jimmy didn't go to university was because _____ Uncle James.

_____ -uncle's wealth was gone. Uncle Clifford had _____ ng the war and his investments soured while _____ e were outstanding taxes on grandmother's _____ rfeited after she died.

When Dad got back to Canada after the war he returned to Edmonton to complete a degree in mining engineering. In his later years he would get together with some of his old college buddies and they would tell stories. After I learned to drive, I became the designated driver and would sit and listen to the old men talk and drink rum. Dad's friend Jim Nicoll told a story about the first Remembrance Day after the war. He and my dad and some other veterans hired a taxi and went to the Strathcona barracks. They tied a cannon to the back of the taxi and had the driver take them to the bank of the North Saskatchewan River. There they filled the cannon with gunpowder, wadded it with newspapers, and fired off a salute in memory of their fallen comrades. When they got back to the university, Dad was summoned to the office of the chancellor, Henry Marshall Tory. Tory told him he had had a complaint from the commanding officer of the Strathcona barracks about a stolen cannon. He simply asked Dad for his assurance that those who had taken it would put it back when they were done with it.

After graduation, Dad was unable to find employment as a mining engineer and one day he met his old school principal from Western Canada College. Dr. McRea was looking for a French teacher. Since Dad was from Quebec, McRea suggested he come to the school to teach French. Dad accepted and he taught at Western Canada College until 1923, when the treasurer absconded with the school funds and the place went bankrupt. It was then taken over by the Calgary Board of Education and continues to this day as Western Canada High School.

Dad couldn't teach at a public school because he did not have a Normal School degree. He later obtained a masters in English, and that qualified him to teach in public schools. In the meantime he tried his hand at farming. He took a piece of Soldier Settlement Act land on the bank of the Pembina River not far from Jarvie, Alberta, a little hamlet about 150 kilometres north of Edmonton. This is where he met my mother.

My mother was born in the town of Courtrai, in West Flanders, Belgium, in 1905. Their family name was Mourtier, but her Uncle

Gus took the name Martin when he came to Canada sometime before the First World War. One story about the name change was just that someone mistranscribed some sloppy handwriting. The other was that Uncle Gus was avoiding the draft. In any event, my mother's family came to join him in 1914. My mother always maintained that they had only come for a visit and had been prevented from going back by the outbreak of the war. My impression is that her parents told her a story to soften the truth, which was that they were emigrating. She stuck to her version of the story all of her life.

I loved my mother, and she was a virtuous woman who devoted her life to her family. However, she often seemed unhappy and was inclined to dwell on negative memories. My father described her as melancholy. If she were alive today, she would likely be diagnosed as clinically depressed. She may have been the reason my father worked so hard to maintain a positive outlook.

In his book *The Weekender Effect* Bob Sandford talks about our human need for place. He tells of the Swiss mercenaries who, when stationed overseas, would be debilitated by things that reminded them of home. This malady was referred to as the "terrible Swiss disease." I think my mother may have been an example of this. She had fond memories of Belgium, where her father had been a baker and they had lived in reasonable comfort. On the homestead at Jarvie, her father worked the farm and worked on the railway to supplement the farm. He was a small man, not cut out for heavy manual labour, and life was hard. She suffered watching him. As if the hardships of life on the homestead were not enough, her older brother, Gaston, died in the great flu epidemic of 1919. My grandmother mourned for him until she died, and I believe my mother mourned her mother's sorrow until she died.

My mother didn't make her marriage to my father sound very romantic. They met in Jarvie, and her mother would often invite the local schoolteacher for dinner. Dad was a friend of the teacher, Red Jamieson, and one day when he was visiting in Jarvie, he was invited to join him at my grandparents' house. Dad was 15 years her senior, but they began a correspondence over the next few years. Then the time came for her to leave home because her parents couldn't afford to keep her. Her only prospect of employment was as a nurse's aide, and she dreaded the thought of it. "So it was either that or marry your father." She married my father.

They were married in Banff in 1929 and took packhorses into the mountains for their honeymoon.

My father, who by then had completed his MA, had been hired by the Town of Athabasca to teach there. When they returned from their wedding trip, however, there was a letter waiting. The town did not have funds to pay him. Dad sometimes said he wished he had just gone anyway and worked for groceries and a place to stay. I wonder how different my life would have been had I grown up on the Athabasca River instead of the Bow.

In any event the ugly practice of nepotism came to Dad's rescue. His brother Jimmy was a political bagman for the then ruling Liberal party of Alberta. There was an opening for a stipendiary magistrate in Waterton Lakes, and Jimmy got my father the job. He had no legal experience, but he had two university degrees and an honourable discharge from the Canadian Army with the rank of lieutenant, so he was probably better qualified than many others who had held the position.

The job lasted until the Liberals lost the next election, never to be elected again in Alberta. The Reillys moved back to Calgary and eventually back into the old family home at 337. Again my mother was in a place she didn't like. The house was never hers, it was her in-laws', and she never seemed to be at home there. After my father died in 1977 I arranged the sale of the house and it was torn down to make room for a parking lot. My mother bought a little house in Windsor Park, and I think the years she lived there were some of the happiest of her life. It was the only place that was really hers.

My parents had five children, of whom I am the youngest. My sister, Mary Furneaux, is 16 years older than I, and I think she is the best sister ever. She is always cheerful and has managed to maintain a positive outlook through all of the difficulties of raising her own family of seven.

I've heard it said that children often have the personality of the parent of the opposite sex. This seems to be true of my sister. She has my father's virtues: his humour and patience, his philosophical outlook.

Unfortunately, my brothers seemed to inherit a mix of my mother's melancholy and my grandfather's bad temper. In many childhood memories I am cringing in fear, hiding while one of my older brothers has given in to a rage that my parents are unable to control. I suppose they have mellowed in their old age, as I have, but I don't see them much anymore.

I like to think I am more like my sister. She was old enough to be my mother. Perhaps she was the mother figure whose personality I inherited.

It was all good training for me. Being the youngest and weakest of my family made me sensitive to the weaknesses of others. It also instilled a contempt for those who abuse their power and authority, and has made me careful to never abuse my power as a judge to bully or put people down. While it is popular to speak of punishing wrongdoers, I think it is more important to understand them. While it is popular to think of wrongdoers as bad people, I believe that the vast majority of those who appear before me in court are just ordinary people who have made mistakes through human weakness.

It also made me careful not to offend anyone. I was always so afraid of saying anything that would trigger one of my brothers' rages that I learned to be very careful about what I said. I had a fear of speaking, but in spite of my self-doubt, I apparently achieved a sufficiently credible reputation among my peers that when I sought the appointment as a judge, I was successful in obtaining it. I was just 30 years old when, on June 21, 1977, I had the distinction of being the youngest Provincial Court judge ever appointed in the history of Alberta.

Admittedly the appointment was not much of a plum back then. The salary was less than $40,000 a year, when some of my former classmates were making over $100,000. I recall attending a house party not long after my appointment. One of the guests was Ken Moore, then the Chief Justice of the Alberta Court of Queen's Bench. He made the comment that he was disappointed to see me take the judgeship because he thought I had a great future at the bar.

I didn't like being a lawyer, though, and one day in about 1975 Judge Gary Cioni suggested I should apply for the judge's position in Drumheller. The post was vacant and was being covered by the Calgary judges. At that time there were only six judges in the Criminal Division of the Provincial Court in Calgary, and covering the extra courts was a significant burden for them. Cioni's suggestion may have been more out of desperation than admiration for my legal aptitude, but I liked the idea. I wrote a letter to the then deputy attorney general, Bill McLean, inquiring about the possibility of receiving the appointment. Nothing ever came of it, except that the letter stayed on file somewhere.

The Provincial Court Act was passed in 1976 and magistrates became Provincial Court judges. The newly formed Provincial Court also had a chief judge, of course, and the first holder of that office was Allan Cawsey.

One day in early 1977 I received a call from Chief Judge Cawsey.

He asked me if I was still interested in an appointment to the court. I told him the prospect appealed to me but I had pretty much forgotten about it. I didn't think I was old enough. He said he was still prepared to invite me to an interview with the Judicial Council if I would attend, and commented that Pitt the Younger had been Prime Minister of England at 24.

I agreed to the interview, still not expecting very much, but again that ugly practice of nepotism may have played a part. My father was one of eight children, all of whom were deceased by 1977. Of all his brothers and sisters, I had one cousin, his brother Jimmy's daughter, Phoebe Maude Reilly. She was referred to as Aunt Maude because she was about 40 years older than I. Her husband was Sydney Wood, the senior partner of the firm of Wood Moir.

The Judicial Council is made up of the chief justice of the Court of Appeal, the chief justice of the Court of Queen's Bench, the chief judge of the Provincial Court, the president of the Law Society, or their designates, and a couple of laymen. On that day, Mr. Justice Arnold Moir was the designate for the Court of Appeal (he was the Moir of Wood Moir). Mr. Justice Cam Steer was the designate for the Court of Queen's Bench and Joe Brumlik was the designate for the Law Society. All had been partners with my Uncle Syd.

I only remember being asked two questions: why did I want to be a judge, and would I still be willing to go to Drumheller.

In answer to the first, I said that I didn't like being one of the adversaries in our adversarial system. I thought my nature was better suited to being a referee.

To the second, I said that I was no longer able to leave Calgary. My father had had a stroke and was hospitalized. I had to stay in Calgary to be with my mother. Justice Moir expressed concern that "Uncle Charlie" was not well (Aunt Maude and Uncle

Syd always referred to my father as Uncle Charlie, and so did everyone else in the firm). My recollection is that the rest of the interview was spent talking about Uncle Charlie.

The council recommended my appointment and it was accepted by the Attorney General, Jim Foster, and signed by Lieutenant-Governor Steinhauer.

I was assigned to the Criminal Division in Calgary, and sat in Calgary until 1981, when rural courts serviced from Calgary were reorganized into the north and south circuits. I was assigned to the north circuit, which consisted of Cochrane, Airdrie and Didsbury. I was the presiding judge for those towns until 1986, when I was reassigned to Calgary.

As I have said, the Stoney Indian reserve lies to the west of the town of Cochrane, and all charges laid on the reserve are heard in Cochrane. The population of the reserve was about 3,500 people, and the area serviced by the court has a total population of about 35,000. "The Stoneys" made up about 75 per cent of the work of the court.

In those five years, from 1981 to 1986, I knew nothing about the Stoney people and it didn't matter. The wisdom of the day was that you treat everyone equally by treating everyone the same. Therefore, you didn't have to know anything about the individuals you were dealing with. I have subsequently come to see this attitude as racism.

❖ 3 ❖

MY ABORIGINAL EDUCATION

In 1992 I learned that the resident judge for Banff/Canmore, Bob Davie, wanted to move to Calgary. We made a joint application to the Attorney General to have our residences redesignated. That request was granted as of May 1, 1993.

At that time, the resident judge for Banff/Canmore sat one day in Canmore and three days in Banff. On my initiative, over the next two years, Banff sittings were reduced to one day a week and I began sitting in Cochrane. In 1996 Cochrane was added to the Banff/Canmore circuit and became part of my full-time assignment.

I look back on the years from 1981 to 1986 with some recrimination. I see myself as an arrogant, rednecked, ignorant white man applying English law to a people whose freedom had been taken from them by my predecessors. I regret my ignorance, but, as I have said, I think the circumstances may have been necessary for my overall education.

In the '80s, I was always happy enough to see the courtroom filled with Indians (that was the term we were still using then). They would all plead guilty and I would glibly hand out sentences of 30 days on drunk charges, six months for repeat drinking drivers, six months to two or three years for wife beating. I was most proud of my ability to get through 30 to 50 cases before lunch. I was the darling of the court because I applied the law with efficiency and I followed the guidelines set out by the Court of Appeal without questioning them.

I don't fret about the sentences I imposed. I have usually tried to err on the side of leniency, and in spite of my efficiency I don't think the sentences were any heavier than any other judge would have imposed. What I do fret about is the fact that these people were just faceless objects to me. Of course, that was the wisdom of the day. A judge was supposed to be "objective."

Between 1986 and 1996 there had been significant changes in the awareness of the plight of the Aboriginal people of Canada in general and their plight in the justice system in particular. In 1991 the government of Alberta created a Task Force on the Canadian Criminal Justice System and Its Impact on the Indian and Métis People of Alberta, chaired by Allan Cawsey. Because Cawsey was the chief judge who had invited me to become a judge, I read the result of the task force's work, the Cawsey Report, with a personal interest.

The task force had visited dozens of Native communities in the province and heard hundreds of submissions. In the report Mr. Justice Cawsey said a couple of things that really hit home with me:

1. Judges who know nothing about the communities in which they sit are seen as "judicial tyrants." I shake my head when I reflect on how accurately that describes the Judge Reilly of the 1980s.

2. If you treat people who are not the same as if they are the same, you are practising "systemic discrimination." This is the "racism" I spoke of at the end of chapter 2. The most important lesson in my judicial career was to learn that "same" is not "equal." I had been a judge for 15 years by that time, and the most important lesson I learned was that *same is not equal.*

After reading the report, I assigned myself the task of getting to know the Stoney people. This was not easy. There was hardly anyone on the reserve whom I hadn't sent to jail or who wasn't related to someone I had sent to jail, so no one was really anxious to talk to me. They don't have a public relations officer or a tourist bureau. It was a little difficult to know where to start. One day, I complained about this difficulty to my friend Jeff Williams. Jeff had been in the area for a long time and had extensive dealings with the Stoneys. He said, "John, we took their land. They don't like you."

Marjorie Powderface was the Native court worker at the time. I have always had a special fondness for Marjorie because she has a child named Riley. I have often said her father, Bert Wildman, was one of my favourite Stoneys. He was a big man who must have been very powerful in his youth. He would give an opinion on something and always conclude with the words "that's how I see it, anyways." To me he was the typical strong but gentle Indian. He had a wealth of knowledge but he would never try to impose his views on anyone. He would simply state them and say, "That's how I see it, anyways." He was one of those elders who deserved the title *elder*, a man who had achieved the wisdom and virtue of a long life well lived.

Bert had a twin sister, Lillie, who died the year before Bert turned 87. The community had celebrated their joint birthday for years, but now the family thought it would be too sad to have the celebration at Morley. So they decided to have it with the Copithorne family at the Jumping Pound hall. I had the honour of speaking at this gathering, and I really enjoyed the stories that others told.

One old rancher told the story of meeting Bert Wildman at the Copithorne ranch and spending a pleasant evening visiting with him. At the end of the evening, as Bert was getting on his horse to ride home, the rancher told him to be careful because they were in "Indian territory."

It was great to see the old man laugh, but I was scared for him.

He was looking old. My father had died shortly after his 87th birthday. Bert reminded me of my dad, and I was afraid he too was getting close to the end.

Bert died just before Christmas. I confused the date of his funeral and thought it was a day later than it was. I was on the reserve helping unload a truck full of Christmas hampers, and one of the Stoneys mentioned that he was leaving to go to Bert's funeral. I was dressed in work clothes – jeans, an old sweat shirt and jacket – and I didn't have time to change. I went to the funeral thinking I would sneak in and sit at the back. Marjorie spotted me and asked me to stand in the receiving line. At Stoney funerals there is a tradition at the end of the ceremony where the people come up to the coffin, pay their last respects and shake hands with immediate family and close friends who stand on either side of the coffin. So there I was beside Marshall Copithorne, who was dressed appropriately for the occasion. I was really embarrassed, but I was sure Bert was having another good laugh at my expense, and that made it okay.

When I had started my quest to get to know the Stoneys, Marjorie Powderface said that if I wanted to do something for them, I could make donations of toys and baby clothes to the Eagles Nest, a shelter for battered women on the reserve. My wife and I had infant children at the time (we have a daughter born in 1993 and a son in 1995). So I would gather up their clothes and toys, and others from friends and relatives, and drop them at the Eagles Nest.

The director of the shelter was Tina Fox. I had made it known that I wanted to learn more about Aboriginal culture in general and about the Stoney people in particular, and Tina arranged for me to attend an inter-services meeting in the health services building in January 1997. Mary Stacey was taking notes. Jack Heynan was giving a presentation on team building. We took a break for coffee. When the meeting reconvened, several of the people who had been present didn't come back. They had been given pink slips during the break. Mary advised she would not be taking notes for rest of meeting because she was no longer employed. This was my first experience with tribal tyranny. Chief John Snow had been re-elected after four years out of office, and he was removing anyone who had served under Chief Ernest Wesley. It was later reported that Snow fired close to a hundred people on his return to power and that he did it without consulting the tribal council.

In the meantime, my efforts to learn about Aboriginal justice were being noted and the Cochrane detachment of the RCMP arranged for me to be invited to a Family Group Conferencing training session in Edmonton from January 21 to 23, 1997. They thought it was appropriate because it had something to do with Aboriginal justice.

David Moore and John McDonald of Transformative Justice Australia moderated the program. They taught a process based on the "healing circle" used by the Māori in New Zealand. I cannot say enough about this program. It was mind altering and life changing. For the first time, I saw a possibility of a justice system that would do more than just lock people up until they got tired of going to jail.

The most inspiring session in the program was devastatingly simple but immensely powerful. We were divided into small groups and asked to discuss why people do the right things and how this can be encouraged, as opposed to why people do wrong and how this can be prevented. The consensus was that people who do the right things are motivated by relationship, self-respect and respect for others.

I had been a judge for almost 20 years, and for the first time I got a bit of an understanding of the term *restorative justice*. It was a most exciting concept. There were provisions that could be understood as restorative justice in the amendments to the Criminal Code of Canada that had come into effect in September of 1996, but I hadn't understood them. In my Eurocentric world view, I thought restorative justice meant that if you break a window, you pay for the repair of the window. What I began to see was deeper and more complicated, but much more powerful. If you break a window, you damage your relationship with the owner of the window and with everyone who is upset by your conduct. The real meaning of restorative justice is the repair of those relationships. The Ojibway, for example, say that a man who behaves badly behaves as if he has no relations.

The program talked about shaming as a method of behaviour modification. It occurred to me that our criminal justice system is based on the assumption that the best way to modify behaviour is to instill fear through punishment or the threat of punishment. This program offered an alternative to punishment. It offered a method of behaviour modification based on relationship, understanding, reconciliation, restitution and even forgiveness. It offered both reduced case loads and lower rates of recidivism. I wanted more and I communicated my enthusiasm to the organizers of the program.

Transformative Justice Australia was to present an information session on Family Group Conferencing at a meeting of the Aboriginal Justice Learning Network to be held in Calgary February 7 and 8, 1997. I requested and received an invitation.

The Aboriginal Justice Learning Network was an initiative created by the federal government to "promote and support the provision of professional, culturally relevant restorative justice services for Aboriginal peoples." The meeting in Calgary was informative and encouraging, but the best thing about it was that I met a Cree activist and medicine woman named Rose Auger.

I will always remember her flamboyant entrance. She was wearing a purple, bolero-style felt jacket and a matching wide-brimmed hat. She was a short, heavy-set woman with piercing, laughing eyes. For some reason she spoke to me. Her smooth olive skin and round face reminded me of my mother, and I immediately liked her. She became my teacher and mentor. I recall our first conversation going something like this:

"Who are you?"

"I'm John Reilly, the judge at Morley."

"What are you going to do?"

"I'm going to fix the Stoneys."

"I will help you. Come and see me. I work with 126 spirits, and I want to do something at Morley, too."

"Where will I find you?"

"I am renting Greg Twoyoungmen's house on the reserve. Do you know where that is?"

"Yes."

"Come to see me, and come for a sweat."

"I will come and see you, but I don't want to do a sweat. I don't even like saunas, and I hear the sweats are worse."

"We won't cook you. We will teach you how to pray."

The Aboriginal Justice Learning Network meeting consisted of a talking circle with about 50 participants. Rose spoke of the influence of the Aboriginal people on the government of Canada. She said that our Confederation was based on the model of the Six Nations of the Iroquois Confederacy but that we missed the most important aspect of it. In the Iroquois tradition the men were chiefs but it was the women who appointed and removed them.

Rose was a powerful woman, a great teacher and a great support to me in my years of conflict that were soon to come.

Part of the work that David Moore and John McDonald were

doing with the RCMP was the training of facilitators who would produce the program for any community that would have at least 20 people take the program. I requested and received a commitment to produce the program at Morley on April 21 to 23, 1997.

I had a Case Management and Stoney Justice Initiatives meeting set up for March 21 and had invited the three newly elected chiefs of the Stoney Nakoda First Nation: John Snow of the Wesley, Henry Holloway of the Chiniki and Philomene Stevens of the Bearspaw.

I was on a roll. I really thought I was going to be able to make a difference in the delivery of justice on the Stoney reserve. I had discovered something powerful and doable and all we had to do was use it. I was so idealistic and naïve. I did not understand that there were people who were more interested in preserving the status quo than in supporting changes that had the potential to make a huge improvement.

My two greatest adversaries in my quest for better justice for the Stoney people were the people I would most have expected to support me. They were my own chief judge, Edward R. Wachowich, and the senior and dominant chief at Morley, the Reverend Dr. Chief John Snow.

❖ 4 ❖

TINA FOX

Tina Fox was the Native court worker in the 1980s when I did my first assignment at Cochrane. By the time I returned in the '90s she had served five terms as a tribal councillor for the Wesley band and she was the director of the Eagles Nest women's shelter at Morley. Tina was one of the first people on the reserve to go beyond high school.

On occasions when I would stop at the Eagles Nest, we would visit. On one of those visits Tina casually mentioned that she was participating in healing circles for Oliver Abraham. I recognized the name because he had been charged with a number of counts of criminal negligence causing death. He was drunk and caused an accident in which a number of people were killed or injured. One of the deceased was Tina's niece, Buffy Kaquitts. The day I saw Buffy's tombstone was a day that changed my life forever, but that comes later.

I was deeply impressed by Tina's attitude. She was dealing with a man who had killed a member of her family and she was praying for him, helping him. Instead of wishing he was dead, she was concerned that he was suicidal as a result of what he had done. I don't think there is a word for forgiveness in her language. In order to forgive, you must first blame, and Indians don't do that. It's like we don't think about forgiving someone who stumbles and falls, for that is just an accident. Oliver Abraham got drunk and killed Buffy Kaquitts. It happened. Now, instead of wanting to punish him, Tina wanted to help him.

I learned that this is a basic difference between Eurocentric justice and the justice concepts of Aboriginal peoples. We see wrongdoing as something that needs to be punished. They see it as illness in need of healing and as ignorance in need of teaching. I say their view is more enlightened. And more productive.

One day after my initial meeting with Tina at the Eagles Nest I called her and asked her to have lunch with me and tell me about Morley. She came and we spent most of the afternoon in conversation. She told me that Morley probably had the highest rates of suicide, children in care, and prescription-drug abuse of any reserve in Alberta. It probably had the highest incidence of alcoholism and domestic violence as well.

I didn't realize it at the time, but Tina Fox is the Mother Theresa of Morley. She was my informant and my ally in the struggle for better conditions on the reserve, and I am privileged to call her my friend. She has devoted her life to helping Stoney children and she has had to overcome her own demons in order to do so. If I ever felt like complaining about my own struggle, I only had to think about Tina to realize how lucky I was.

Tina stood by me, publicly supporting my criticism of the tribal government and John Snow, and she was one of the members of the council. As I've said, she had been the Native court worker in Cochrane in 1981 and 1982, but that was during my years of total ignorance and I don't believe I even talked to her in those years. When I was again assigned to the Cochrane court in 1996 my point of view had changed. In the 1980s I would go to Cochrane directly from Calgary and didn't even know where Morley was. By 1993 we had moved to Canmore and I would drive through the reserve to get to Cochrane. I was still a little confused by the name: Morley is a hamlet on Highway 133X, while the whole reserve is also referred to as Morley.

Tina was born at Morley on Valentine's day 1941. Her mother

died when she was very young and she was raised by her grand-mother. She was sexually abused by an uncle and went through many years of alcohol abuse trying to drown the memories of the childhood that was taken from her. But in spite of the misery of her childhood, Tina has an easy laugh and a beautiful smile. She maintained her cheerful disposition through many more difficulties – the death of her son Moses in 1986 and of her husband, Kent, in 1998. Moses died in a single-vehicle crash, and Tina says she thinks it was a suicide. Kent died of Lou Gehrig's disease. In the last couple of years Tina has survived breast cancer and open-heart surgery.

She was a student at the Indian residential school at Morley and had reached Grade 10 by 1958. She says the Morley students were a few years behind those in off-reserve schools because they had to take Grades 1, 1A and 1B. She remembers Mr. George Thiessen as the teacher who made a difference in her life. He told her she had the ability to go further and she did. She did upgrading at Mount Royal College and then took a nurse's assistant course in 1960. She worked in a number of hospitals over the next eight years, including Gleichen, Alberta; Sheet Harbour, Nova Scotia; and the Holy Cross in Calgary.

Tina's children – Terry, Moses, Kim, Neesha and Trent – were born in 1964, '68, '69, '73 and '76.

In the fall of 1976 Tina Fox was elected to the tribal council, the first woman to hold the position. Prior to running for council, she had held the post of band manager, and it was on her watch that the militant American Indian Movement had attempted an armed occupation of the band office, demanding financial accountability. After the incident ended there were some who believed Tina was behind it. She had been openly critical of tribal government spending, and the fact that her sisters Evangeline Rider and Georgie Chiniquay were part of the occupation would have contributed to the impression that she was involved.

Tina laughed when she told me how she had been at work the day the occupation started. A young Native who was not a Stoney walked into her office with a rifle and told her to get out of the building. She said she told the boy he was on her land and she wasn't moving, so he could go ahead and shoot her if he wanted to. She laughed even more when she recounted that he had just walked out rather than argue with her. The occupation ended peacefully, with government promises to investigate the complaints. The investigation resulted in charges being laid against the chiefs and council, but they pleaded "tribal custom" and there were no convictions.

Over the next 20 years Tina served five two-year terms on council. After being director of the Eagles Nest during 1996, she was re-elected to council for the 1997/98 term. This was the same time that John Snow regained office after four years during which Ernest Wesley had been chief.

The year 1997 must have been one of the worst ever on the Stoney reserve. Snow's return to office followed 22 consecutive years as chief, from 1970 to 1992. Those 22 years had apparently given him a sense of entitlement. On his return he fired practically everyone who had worked for the band during his absence, including those hired by his own administration prior to 1992.

Throughout all of this, Tina Fox seemed to maintain her sense of humour, but her easy smile and infectious laugh covered her firm resolve to help her people and her courage to do so at whatever personal cost to herself.

❖ 5 ❖

THE REVEREND DOCTOR
CHIEF JOHN SNOW

On March 21, 1997, we had a Case Management & Stoney Justice Initiatives meeting in the boardroom at the Cochrane Provincial Building. There were representatives from the Department of Justice, legal aid, probation, Native counselling, the police, a number of lawyers and the three Stoney chiefs: John Snow, Philomene Stevens and Henry Holloway.

I was looking forward to meeting Chief Snow. I was still impressed by his reputation as one of the most outstanding chiefs in Canada, an ordained minister in the United Church and the recipient of two honorary doctorates from the University of Calgary. What impressed me also was that he had been the keynote speaker at a national convention of the Canadian Bar Association.

We shook hands outside of the boardroom and chatted briefly. I attempted to make light conversation and told Snow I felt I had some connection with his people because my father had been a good friend of John Laurie. Snow said something negative about Laurie and I let the subject drop. I was beginning to dislike him.

I also remember the hair standing up on the back of my neck when I shook his hand. It was an eerie feeling. I have since come to the conclusion that I was being touched by the most evil man I have ever encountered. Many Stoneys will refuse to shake the hand of a man they believe to be a medicine man, especially one they believe practises bad medicine.

We went into the boardroom, where the chairs were arranged for a talking circle. I went to the far end of the room and sat down. Snow sat closest to the door, with Philomene Stevens on one side and Henry Holloway on the other.

Henry was the most reasonable of the three. He likely would have done some good things for his people had it not been for the circumstances in which he found himself.

Philomene Stevens was a morbidly obese little woman who was said to have a Grade 4 education. It is possible she didn't even know how to read. Her father, John Stevens, had a reputation as a medicine man. He had made money selling timber during the summer of 1996 when hundreds of logging trucks were taking away load after load from the Stoney reserve. Ernest Wesley had initiated litigation to stop these sales and force payment to the tribal administration from the proceeds. There is a big bare spot on a hillside to the south of the Trans-Canada Highway, a few miles west of the access road to Morley, which is referred to as the "John Stevens clear-cut." It is likely that Philomene's election as chief was due in large part to money paid out by her father. One of the first acts of the new council was to discontinue the lawsuit.

After everyone in the room had introduced themselves, I welcomed the chiefs and told them that I was concerned about the disproportionate number of Stoneys that were appearing in the court in Cochrane. I said I would like to work with the tribal council to establish programs that might help their people deal with the underlying problems that brought them into conflict with the law.

I said I would like to help create a justice program in which volunteers from the community could participate in suggesting culturally appropriate dispositions that might be beneficial to the whole community. I don't specifically recall whether I spoke about Family Group Conferencing, but I likely did. It was my firm conviction that if justice were ever going to mean anything for the Stoney people, they would have to be involved in the system.

Snow told me that there was no funding available for programs, that the previous council had left the reserve deep in debt, and that no one on the reserve could afford to do volunteer work. He said even he didn't have money to buy gas to drive across the reserve during the years he was out of office. (This wasn't true. He had a paying position with the Assembly of First Nations during those years.)

Holloway and Stevens said they supported Chief Snow, and with that they left the meeting. I was somewhat deflated. Here I was, the local judge, presiding over hundreds of cases involving their people, offering to help them help their people, and they just "blew me off."

Snow, in theory, was just one of three chiefs, and in theory each had equal authority. The Stoney people are divided into three groups: the Wesley, the Chiniki and the Bearspaw. In 1997 they still referred to this as three "bands" making up one "tribe." Now they refer to each of the groups as a First Nation: the Wesley First Nation, the Chiniki First Nation and the Bearspaw First Nation. I believe this division is one of the most serious obstacles to social development on the reserve, and I will speak more about this later. Whenever I have occasion to write to the chiefs, I address each of them as chief of their division of the Stoney Nakoda Nation.

Although Snow was just one of three chiefs, he had dominated the reserve from the time of his first election. As a result of his diploma from Cook College & Theological School in Tempe, Arizona, which he obtained in 1963, he had the advantage of being better educated than any of his fellow chiefs. He had also been the only chief of the Wesley band in those years, whereas the Chiniki and Bearspaw had elected various people as their chiefs. Snow was therefore the most senior and most experienced chief and the other chiefs would defer to him.

It was obvious at that meeting that he was in total control. The governance of the reserve at that time, and for as long as Snow had been chief, was by what they called "the three chiefs committee." Each of the bands elected a chief and four councillors. The tribal council consisted of the three chiefs and the 12 councillors, but the councillors were in an advisory role only. All governing authority was in the three chiefs committee. Snow, by virtue of his seniority, and his ability to manipulate at least one of the other chiefs, could virtually act as a dictator.

It was easy to imagine that John Snow could control Philomene Stevens's vote. From my observation of her, she must have thought she was sitting next to God himself when she sat next to John Snow.

I subsequently said in my written judgment in the Hunter case that Snow ruled the reserve like the dictator of a banana republic. I understand that this comment offended him. Later, when asked how he felt about me, he replied: "How would you feel about someone who compared you to the dictator of a banana republic?"

Notwithstanding my disappointment in the Case Management & Stoney Justice Initiatives meeting, I still had the Family Group Conferencing program scheduled for Nakoda Lodge in April. I wanted to discuss this with Chief Snow because I wanted to get his permission to use the lodge. I phoned him at least a half a dozen times and his assistant told me each time that he was away. Once she told me he was in Seattle, once in Montreal and other times in other places. It seemed apparent that lack of funds was not interfering with his travel budget.

Some time after that meeting I had occasion to visit with Ken Soldier, who had been the Chiniki chief prior to Henry Holloway.

I told him what Chief Snow had said about being left with a big debt. Soldier said it was a lie, that there was over a million-dollar surplus in the education department alone.

Ken Soldier was someone I considered to be one of my greatest success stories. In the '70s and '80s he had had a serious problem with alcohol and had been a frequent attender in the court at Cochrane on drunk charges. I don't know how many times I had sentenced him to 30 days for being drunk, but on the last time he appeared in court as an accused, he pleaded guilty and I asked him, "So, do you want to go back to jail, or do you want to take the treatment? If you want to do the treatment, I can put you on probation; you'll be required to spend 28 days at the medicine lodge and abstain from alcohol for two years."

I really expected him to just take the 30 days. He looked like he was in terrible pain from a hangover. He seemed to think about the choice, and then he said, "I'll take the treatment."

He went to the medicine lodge, sobered up and then worked there as a counsellor for a number of years. He was subsequently elected Chiniki chief and as chief he had attended a Case Management & Stoney Justice Initiatives meeting I had convened in 1996. Ken was enthusiastic about my ambition to create justice programs for the Stoneys, but his health was failing. Diabetes, aggravated by years of alcohol abuse, had caught up with him. He now used a wheelchair and needed regular dialysis. He lost the election in 1996. He told me he was afraid he might because people were concerned that his health would not allow him to do the job.

Ken and I became friends. Ironic, in view of the number of times I had sent him to jail, but that is the Stoney way, at least among the older generation.

A few days before Ken died, Marjorie Powderface came and told me, "The elder Ken Soldier is in the hospital and he wants to see you." I went as soon as I was able. He was so weak he couldn't sit up but he shifted a bit and said, "I just wanted to say goodbye." We visited for a short time but he was too tired and weak for much conversation. He died the next day.

I was honoured when asked to speak at his funeral. I had a difficult time choking back tears when I did so.

When Ken told me there was a surplus at the end of his tenure, and Snow told me there was a deficit, I had no doubt about which statement was the truth. Ken Soldier seemed genuinely interested in doing something for his people. From what I saw of Snow, he didn't even pretend to care about them.

❖ 6 ❖

MARLON HOUSE

Sometime in 1978 Sandra Dixon met Marlon House at a dance. House asked her to go out with him. She refused because she was married. He continued to pursue her. On January 1, 1979, she agreed and they went out. He took her home to Morley and kept her there for three months. During that time she was regularly beaten. On one occasion he bent her finger back so far that it broke. He refused to allow her to get medical care. The finger never did heal properly. Seventeen years later House was charged with unlawful confinement and assault causing bodily harm in relation to these events.

Vivian Goodrunning lived with him for six years from 1981 to 1986, had three of his children, was regularly beaten and not allowed to visit her family or speak to anyone except under very strict control. Ten years later House was charged with her unlawful confinement and assault.

Retillia Rabbit could be described as an unwilling house guest for a few weeks in the spring of 1992 and would probably never have been the subject of charges against House except for the other women he abused.

House was charged with the unlawful confinement of Cynthia Beaver from December 1992 until May 1996, and she was still with him at the time of trial in November 1996. I convicted on this charge in spite of Cynthia's testimony that she loved him and wanted to be with him. The Court of Appeal reversed this conviction. I will comment later about my view of their decision.

On reviewing the transcript of the trial I heard in November of 1996, for the purpose of writing this book, I now think I missed the enormity of the offences committed against Vivian Goodrunning. I was focused on whether or not the charges before me were established. I missed the big picture.

Vivian was a good witness and I had no difficulty believing what she said. She had endured years of abuse. I believe that her years of suffering had taken away the ability to express emotion. I accepted that it was only as a result of a successful treatment program that she was able to talk about it at all. Her matter-of-fact description of the events belied the emotion and horror of her experience. I heard her evidence as a judge should – dispassionately and critically examining it for probative value, looking for inconsistencies and improbabilities that might be the reasonable doubt that would require me to acquit the accused.

Admittedly, I began the trial with considerable skepticism about the Crown's case. The first counts on the information were 17 years old. My initial reaction was that the prosecutor's office must not have had enough work to do if they were dredging up domestic abuse cases going back so far. But the seriousness of the Crown's intention became evident with the first witness, Vivian Goodrunning.

Vivian was born on February 7, 1967, on the Sunchild reserve. The reserve is 60 kilometres northwest of Rocky Mountain House, Alberta, and has a population of fewer than a thousand. It is located in the wilderness on the eastern slopes of the Rocky Mountains and is very isolated. It is easy to imagine the naïve wonderment of 14-year-old Vivian when she went to Rocky for the wedding of her uncle, Nelson Day Chief. This was on February 28, 1981.

Marlon House was playing in the band at the wedding dance. He was 31 years old. Vivian said she didn't know how it happened but a few weeks later she was on her way to Morley to live with Marlon and his family. She evidently felt some attraction for him, as she had "just kept thinking about him all the time" in those intervening weeks.

However, it was only a few days after she arrived that Marlon beat her, the first of the assaults that would become a regular part of her life for the next six years. She said it was because he thought she was "going after" one of his brothers.

On one occasion, before the birth of Vivian's first child, her mother came and got her and took her to her aunt's in Onoway, Alberta. She was only there a few days when Marlon found her and she returned to Morley with him. When asked why she went with him, she said she did not know, but throughout her evidence she said she did what he said because she was afraid of him.

Her first child, Kimberly, was born when Vivian was 15. She was pregnant again about six or seven months later when Marlon beat her with his fists, stabbed her twice in the leg and once in the head, and left her bleeding and unconscious on the kitchen floor. She awoke to find Kimberly on top of her and covered in her (Vivian's) blood. She crawled to the bathroom to clean herself and put tobacco on her wounds to stop the bleeding. She said she believed this beating caused the miscarriage of her second child.

Vivian left House a second time when she was in her third month of pregnancy with Andrew, and stayed with her mother at Sunchild for about 10 months. Then Marlon came again, told her he would change, that he would be a good father, and she agreed to go back with him. She said she did not have a father when she was growing up, and therefore wanted her children to have one.

As soon as they were back at Morley he beat her again. She had named the baby Andrew Michael Roy House. He accused her of having the baby with his brother, Roy, and naming it after him. In this beating he kicked her in the head with steel-toed boots, leaving a scar inside her right eyebrow, in the middle of her forehead.

The saddest part of Vivian's story is her daughter, Marlena. She said she left this child with her mother because "she wasn't made the way a baby should be made"; "he raped me"; "and it hurt so much"; and "it's all horrible, like it keeps coming back to me, every time when I look at her. That's why I told my mom to keep her."

Vivian Goodrunning's final release from Marlon House came when her mother enlisted the help of the RCMP to get her out of Morley. How could she have stayed for six years and gone back more or less voluntarily on the first two occasions when her mother brought her back?

She was only 14 when this started. She spent the next six years under his absolute control. They lived in a trailer close to Marlon's mother's house. When he left in the morning he would take her to his mother's house and get her back when he came home. She was not allowed to talk with anyone, including her own family. She must have lived in continual fear. But she said that even the last time she left she wanted to go back and believed it was because of "bad medicine."

This created a huge problem for me. He's charged with her unlawful confinement, but she wants to go back to him and says she can't get away because he's using medicine. Its easy to imagine the reaction in the Court of Appeal if I were to say I found him guilty of the charge of unlawful confinement because he did, by the use of bad medicine, hold her against her will. I wonder if a court composed of people who grew up in the same tradition would take a different view. Our society professes to believe in God. Atheists seem to be in the minority. Yet any suggestion that something has a spiritual cause is scoffed at.

Photini Papadatou was the Crown prosecutor in the case. Fourteen years after the House trial I asked her if she remembered anything about it and she said she remembered it clearly. She said she remembered Marjorie Powderface wanting her to have rat root to protect herself from the bad medicine and asking to have the courtroom locked until the proceedings began each day. House was out on bail during the trial and he would go into the courtroom and walk up and down the rows of seats before court was called to order. The women were afraid he was putting bad medicine in the courtroom.

Photini is Greek. She said her people have many similar beliefs and so she was quite prepared to accept the reality of which Marjorie was speaking. This belief, in Native spirituality, is that the spirits of the dead continue to have an influence on the living. In some cases control by those spirits can be devastating. It is believed that people who do wrong do so because bad spirits are controlling them.

This belief may make it a terrifying experience for a Native person to give evidence in a judicial proceeding, because part of the belief is that if you confront a wrongdoer, you also confront the evil spirit that is making him misbehave and you may bring that evil upon yourself.

In my Irish upbringing we were never allowed to speak of the devil. My father firmly believed that doing so might summon him. In our culture generally in Canada, when a person's name is mentioned in conversation and that person arrives, you often hear someone say "speak of the devil…" The whole of that expression is "speak of the devil and the devil will come." When my father would hear that comment, he would softly suggest that a better expression would be "speak of the angels…"

In the sweat lodges, the participants pray to the grandmothers and grandfathers. They believe that the spirits of their departed relations will give them help in dealing with their difficulties. This is much the same as the spirituality I grew up with, and I believe my father's spirit and that of his old friend John Laurie have been with me in the sweat lodges of the Stoney.

So I have wrestled with what I believe about bad medicine in relation to Marlon House. The following is an excerpt from the trial transcript where Photini's examination of the witness Vivian Goodrunning deals with the matter of medicine:

Q   Okay. And is that why you think you kept going back?
A   Yes.

Q   And the medicine man that your mom took you to, what did he do?
A   He cured me to get him off my mind.

Q   Okay. After you went to the medicine man, after your mom took you to the medicine man, did you want to go back?
A   No.

Q   Okay. Did you have to go more than once to the medicine man to cure you?
A   I went twice.

Q   Okay. Why did you go twice?
A   'Cause the first one, the first time, that person couldn't do it, so I went to someone else, and ...

Q   And did it work the second time?
A   Yeah.

Q   Okay. And ever since you went to the medicine man the second time, have you gone back?
A   No.

Q   Now, did you also go and see a counsellor when you left the accused? Did you go and talk to someone about the stuff that happened to you?

A   No, I hid it for a long time.

Q   How long was it before you could talk about it?
A   Since – since last year is when I went to treatment centre.

Q   Okay. You were telling us earlier about your child Marlena and that she has to stay with your mother but she doesn't under-stand why she has to stay with your mother. Can you tell us why you sent your child Marlena to stay with your mother?
A   'Cause she wasn't made – she wasn't made the proper way a child should be made.

Q   How was she made?
A   He raped me.

Q   Okay. And that's how Marlena was made?
A   Yes. And it hurt so much.

Q   Okay.
A   Every time when I look at her, the memories come back. I know it's been a long time, but ... It's all horrible, like it keeps coming back to me every time when I look at her. That's why I told my mom to keep her.

Q   Okay. When you were with the accused ... you told us in the six years you only saw your family three or four times; is that right?
A   Yes.

Q   Did you try to see your family?
A   I always wanted to see my family.

Q   Okay. Would the accused let you see your family?
A   No.

Q   Was the accused drinking when he lived with you?
A   Yes.

Q   Did he drink the whole six years?

A   Yes.

Q   Did he have a problem with alcohol?

A   Yes.

Q   Has the accused said anything to you about these charges before you came to court?

A   Yes.

Q   What did he say to you?

A   He tried to make a deal with me.

Q   Okay. What did he say to you?

A   He said he would give me back my oldest daughter if I didn't come to this court and testify, and he said if he wins he said he's going to sue me.

Q   Okay. What did you say to him when he said those things to you?

A   I told him I wasn't afraid of him. He thinks – he thinks – he thinks nothing ever happened in our relationship. He thinks everything is just okay ...

The last of House's victims was Cynthia Beaver, though she didn't see it that way at the time and the Court of Appeal didn't either.

Cynthia was born on the reserve at Morley on October 1, 1967. She had had four children before she met Marlon House. They were ages 8, 6, 3, and 3 months when she began living with him.

Before Cynthia was called to the witness stand, a number of her relatives and co-workers testified. They described her before and after she had gone with House. Before, she was a happy-go-lucky, bubbly, friendly woman. She cared for her children. The only times she was late or absent from work were when she had problems with babysitters, because she would not leave the children with "just anybody."

After being with House she changed dramatically. She lost weight to the point where she looked emaciated. She often displayed bruises. When she was seen in public she kept her head down and would not speak to any of her old friends. She left her children with her mother and had nothing to do with them.

In May of 1995, after her family expressed concerns about her health, the Cochrane RCMP stopped the school bus House was driving and found Cynthia in the seat behind him. She was wearing a heavy fall or winter coat with the hood pulled down over her face. She was subsequently apprehended under a mental health warrant and taken to Foothills Hospital, where she was kept for several weeks.

House was charged with her unlawful confinement, but she went back to him after her stay in hospital. She was with him at the time of trial and did not attend court. Crown counsel Papadatou applied for a witness warrant on the basis that there had been approximately 20 attempts to serve Cynthia that had been unsuccessful and she appeared to be evading service.

I granted the warrant and Cynthia was brought into court in custody the next day. She was one of the most pathetic-looking people I had ever seen. Photini told me later that someone had commented, "You don't have to call her as a witness, just mark her as an exhibit." This bit of black humour was devastatingly accurate.

When Cynthia's mother testified, she showed a picture of Cynthia with her children. There was almost no resemblance between the healthy, happy-looking woman in the picture and the spectre that stood in the witness box.

Cynthia testified that Marlon House was her husband and she wanted to be with him. She said she gave her children to welfare because they were unwanted babies. She said she didn't want to go back to her damn mother.

In my view the evidence that she was being wrongfully held and maliciously controlled by the accused was overwhelming. She spoke like a zombie, and her physical condition and demeanour established beyond any doubt in my mind that she was the victim of the same kind of abuse as Vivian Goodrunning.

I convicted House on all counts and imposed sentences totalling 15 years in prison:

❖ in relation to Sandra Dixon, three years for the unlawful confinement, and three years concurrent for the assault causing bodily harm;

❖ in relation to Vivian Goodrunning, six years for the unlawful confinement and six years concurrent for the assault causing bodily harm;

❖ in relation to Retillia Rabbit, one year concurrent with the other sentences imposed;

❖ in relation to Cynthia Beaver, five years for the unlawful confinement;

❖ the sentences in relation to Dixon, Goodrunning and Beaver to be served consecutively.

The defence appealed all convictions and sentences. The Court of Appeal read the transcript and said the conviction in relation to Cynthia Beaver was wrong. They set it aside, automatically eliminating that five-year sentence, and said the other sentences were likely longer than they would have been had I not convicted in relation to Cynthia. The court did not give reasons. I guess they just thought it was silly to convict a man of unlawful confinement when the victim says she wants to be with him.

On the sentence appeals, the court reduced the three years re Sandra Dixon to two and the six years re Vivian Goodrunning to five. The concurrent sentence in relation to Retillia Rabbit did not affect the global sentence and was not changed. The court said I had likely imposed harsher sentences because I viewed the whole situation as a continuing pattern over the whole period. Having set aside the conviction re Beaver, they found that this was not so. The sentences remained consecutive, resulting in a net sentence of seven years.

A few years after the trial, I was sitting in the Chiniki Restaurant at Morley, having my usual tea and bannock, when I heard a soft voice say to me: "I paid for your tea and bannock."

It was Cynthia Beaver.

"Why would you pay for my tea and bannock? The last time I saw you I said you were lying and I sent that husband you loved so much to the penitentiary for 15 years."

"I know. You were right. It just took me a long time to break the hold he had on me."

"How did that happen? Did you go to a medicine man like Vivian did?"

"No, something he said at a parole hearing just changed everything for me."

At the trial, I had had no difficulty disbelieving Cynthia. The evidence of her mother and Mary Stacey had convinced me that she was being held against her will and that she was being abused. I had no expert evidence about Stockholm syndrome, but I was satisfied from my observation of her that she was not able to speak freely, and that she was not staying with House from a freely given choice. Whether he was controlling her by bad medicine or by some other kind of mind control, I absolutely believed that he was keeping her against her will, or if not against her will, that he had been able to destroy her will.

Courts of appeal give lip service to the principle that a trial judge hears the witness in person, has the opportunity to make observations that will not be evident in a transcript, and therefore should be given great deference when his findings are challenged. I had watched Cynthia Beaver testify. She was a frightened, emaciated little woman who spoke as if she were in a trance. I had heard the anguish in her mother's voice as she testified about the complete change in her daughter's personality. I had seen Mary Stacey's concern for her co-worker and her conviction that Cynthia was being held against her will and abused. I had listened to the accused testify and had been disgusted by his arrogance, his obvious contempt for his victims and his implausible explanations of their injuries.

I don't usually fret about the Court of Appeal. Sentencing human beings, no matter how bad they are, is a very onerous responsibility. When the Court of Appeal changes a sentence, they are responsible for it, and I have often taken comfort in that. My disappointment in this case, and other cases involving Aboriginal people, is my inability to have the higher court see what I see in my court.

Back at the Chiniki Restaurant, Cynthia Beaver wouldn't talk about medicine.

❖ 7 ❖

ERNEST HUNTER

On New Years Eve 1996 Ernest Hunter and his common-law wife, Rondi Lefthand, went to a party and consumed alcohol. On returning home they quarrelled. The argument became physical and ended in Hunter knocking Lefthand to the floor and kicking her in the head and body. Lefthand suffered cuts and bruising to her face and bruises to her body. The bruising to her face was so bad that she was unrecognizable.

Hunter was born at Morley in 1955. His grandmother raised him until he was 14. When she died, he went to live with his mother, Lavina Brown, and stayed there until he was 18. In 1974 he received the first of his 14 convictions for drinking and driving. He was 19. By 1996 he had been sentenced to more than five years in prison on alcohol-related crimes. On his last conviction for drinking and driving he had been given a curative discharge on 18 months probation with provisions for alcohol treatment.

On receiving that discharge, he attended a 28-day treatment program at Crowfoot Lodge and lived in Calgary for the next two years. During this time he was living with the victim, Rondi Lefthand. According to the submission of his lawyer, he had remained sober and attended AA meetings while he was in Calgary, but he moved back to Morley in the fall of 1996 and fell into the old crowd on the reserve and began drinking again. The drinking continued until the fateful New Years Eve party that led to the assault.

On January 28, 1997, Hunter pleaded not guilty and the matter was set down for trial on May 27, 1997. When he appeared on May 27 he changed his plea to guilty. The facts were read and admitted, a finding of guilt was entered, a presentence report was ordered and the matter was adjourned to June 26 for sentencing.

There is no question that it was a brutal assault. The Court of Appeal decision in *R. v. Brown, Highway and Umphreville* was the case authority that covered the situation and it directed a sentence in the range of 18 months. There is likewise no question that if this had come before me in the '80s I would have listened to the submissions of the defence and then sentenced Hunter to 18 months, probably without even asking the Crown to make submissions.

But it wasn't the '80s; it was the '90s. My world view was changing and hopefully expanding for the better. I was no longer willing to just glibly apply the law and assess a sentence that would satisfy the Court of Appeal. I was now thinking more about the human element that was involved, and I was no longer prepared to just "apply the law."

The law had also changed. Before 1996 there had been no provisions in the Criminal Code of Canada to direct judges in relation to sentencing. The Code sets out each offence and prescribes the maximum penalty in terms of fines and imprisonment. Judges prior to 1996 relied only on precedent, that is, the law as set out in all of the cases that have been decided in the past.

Among the 1996 amendments to the Criminal Code in relation to sentencing guidelines were sections 718, 718.1 and 718.2. They read as follows (as further amended in later years):

> 718. The fundamental purpose of sentencing is to contribute, along with crime prevention initiatives, to respect for the law and the maintenance of a just, peaceful and safe society by imposing just sanctions that have one or more of the following objectives:

(a) to denounce unlawful conduct;

(b) to deter the offender and other persons from committing offences;

(c) to separate offenders from society, where necessary;

(d) to assist in rehabilitating offenders;

(e) to provide reparations for harm done to victims or to the community; and

(f) to provide a sense of responsibility in offenders, and acknowledgment of the harm done to victims and to the community.

718.1 A sentence must be proportionate to the gravity of the offence and the degree of responsibility of the offender.

718.2 A court that imposes a sentence shall also take into consideration the following principles:

(a) a sentence should be increased or reduced to account for any relevant aggravating or mitigating circumstances relating to the offence or the offender, and, without limiting the generality of the foregoing,

　(i) evidence that the offence was motivated by bias, prejudice or hate based on race, national or ethnic origin, language, colour, religion, sex, age, mental or physical disability, sexual orientation, or any similar factor,

　(ii) evidence that the offender, in committing the offence, abused the offender's spouse or common-law partner,

　(ii.1) evidence that the offender, in committing the offence, abused a person under the age of eighteen years,

(iii) evidence that the offender, in committing the
offence, abused a position of trust or authority in
relation to the victim,

(iv) evidence that the offence was committed for the
benefit of, at the direction of or in association with
a criminal organization, or

(v) evidence that the offence was a terrorism offence

shall be deemed to be aggravating circumstances;

(b) a sentence should be similar to sentences imposed
on similar offenders for similar offences committed in
similar circumstances;

(c) where consecutive sentences are imposed, the
combined sentence should not be unduly long or harsh;

(d) an offender should not be deprived of liberty, if
less restrictive sanctions may be appropriate in the
circumstances; and

(e) all available sanctions other than imprisonment that are
reasonable in the circumstances should be considered
for all offenders, with particular attention to the
circumstances of aboriginal offenders.

The last nine words of subsection 718.2(e) – "with particular
attention to the circumstances of Aboriginal offenders" – in my
view, opened the door to a whole new approach to the sentencing of
Aboriginal offenders. This was a new deal created by the Parliament
of Canada. In my career as a judge I had often been required to
apply provisions that I disliked. I particularly dislike minimum sentences because they often cause unfair results. Here, for a change,
was a piece of legislation that I felt was tremendously enlightened.

Jim Ogle, Hunter's lawyer, referred to subsection 718.2(*e*) and lamented that there were no guidelines from the Court of Appeal interpreting the new provisions. While he agreed the case law would call for incarceration, he wondered what effect the new provisions should have.

The amendments to the Criminal Code also included victim impact statements, but those provisions were not yet being implemented and there was no victim impact statement in this case. In the spirit of the new provisions and with my newly acquired appreciation of the Aboriginal preference for decision by consensus, I asked the victim:

"... was there anything you wanted to say?"

"You don't spend two years out of your life with somebody and not care for them. Yes, obviously I still care for him but I'm not ready to continue a relationship with him. But he does have extensive alcohol problems and if you deal with those he'll eventually, you know, be a good person. He was a good person. But it's the alcohol that gets in everybody's life and has ruined everything."

"So what do you think should happen?"

"I think he should have extensive alcoholic, you know, treatment. You know, he needs to go for that. He needs to also do other programs like anger management and stuff like that."

The presentence report acknowledged the lengthy record but indicated that it reflected Hunter's problem with alcohol and that there was hope for him. He had reconciled with a former common-law partner, Alice Beaver, they were living in an alcohol-free household, and his prospects for sobriety appeared favourable. Mr. Ogle told me he had arranged for Hunter to attend an anger management course in Calgary and that he had been doing well there until the tribal council discontinued funding for the course.

Ernest Hunter may not have been the ideal individual for a test case, but his *circumstances* were. He had been doing well for two years before going back to the reserve, where social conditions got him right back into drinking again. He was amenable to treatment and had had some success, but there was no program on the reserve. The Stoney Medicine Lodge, where Ken Soldier had found the sobriety that lasted for the rest of his life, was no longer operating. The biggest red flag to me was that the tribal council had cut off Hunter's funding.

As I say, Hunter was not the perfect choice for a test case on the new Criminal Code principles of sentencing in relation to Aboriginal offenders, but that is how I used him. His case simply came before me when I was in the midst of my quest for better justice for his people, and I did what I believed would contribute to a better understanding of his plight and the plight of the Stoneys. I was doing what I thought would best contribute to the just, peaceful and safe society as set out in the preamble to section 718.

In that month between May 27 and June 26, 1997, I thought of little else besides the reserve and what could be done to change the horrible conditions there. What mostly gnawed at me was the comment about the anger management program. Hunter could not complete it because the tribal council had withdrawn his funding. His victim forgave him and wanted him to get treatment. The presentence report prepared by the Tsuu T'ina Nation/Stoney Corrections Society said his prognosis was favourable. He had the support of a partner and his family. There seemed to be hope for him.

I believed that sending Hunter to jail was a futile exercise that would just waste the resources of the prison system and aggravate rather than alleviate the underlying problems that caused his criminal behaviour. I believed that his offence was the natural product of the dysfunctional community in which he had been born and where he had spent most of his life. I believed that to give effect to the phrase in the new sentencing provisions "to contribute to the maintenance of a just, peaceful and safe society," I had to do more than just send Hunter to jail. I had to set out "the circumstances of [the] Aboriginal offender" which I thought were relevant to his case.

I had no doubt, and I still have no doubt, that the best way to contribute to the maintenance of a just, peaceful and safe society was to impose a sentence that would give Ernest Hunter the treatment he needed. I also knew that the Court of Appeal would not share my idealistic views. The court is made up of men and women who are learned in the law, and the law demands punishment. The precedents were clear. This was a case requiring a term of imprisonment. But if the court knew what was going on in this community – the extent of the violence and dysfunction, the political corruption and financial mismanagement that contributed to that dysfunction and perpetuated it by failing to address it – if I could put these things on the record, the Court of Appeal might see the problems a man like Hunter was facing. They might see the problem the way I was seeing it, and they might agree with my conclusion as to how to deal with it.

❖ 8 ❖

THE WESLEY CEMETERY

One day, a few weeks after the House trial, I was walking down the main street in Cochrane and by chance I met Mary Stacey.

"Mary, how are you? Have you found a job since that fateful meeting I attended?"

"Oh, yes, I'll survive."

"Mary, could you introduce me to people who can tell me what's really happening on the reserve? I had a meeting to talk about justice initiatives. John Snow and the other chiefs came but they say they don't have money and can't do anything about the justice programs I would like to see created."

"They're lying about the money. That reserve has an income of $100-million a year. They just want to spend it on themselves and they don't want any outside interference."

"So tell me more."

"I'll arrange a meeting."

A few days later we met in the basement of the United church in Cochrane. This had its irony. It became a Snow-bashing meeting, and Snow was a United Church minister.

Mary had invited Warren and Mary Anna Harbeck, Ernest and Belva Wesley and Greg Twoyoungmen.

Warren Harbeck is the only non-Stoney I know who can speak the Stoney language. He came to the Stoney reserve in the 1970s to learn the language so he could translate the Bible into it. He had worked as a consultant to John Snow for several years but had a falling out with him because of the number of suicides among the young people and Snow's failure to take any action to deal with it.

Mary Anna had taught school on the reserve for years but had recently been fired in the purge that took place when Snow regained power.

Ernest Wesley had been the Wesley chief from 1992 to 1996.

Belva was Ernest's wife and also a teacher. She had been part of the SITE program, Self Improvement Through Education, that Ernest had established during his tenure as chief.

Greg Twoyoungmen had been a political activist and opponent of Snow since the '70s. Today he is working on a master's degree and is the director of post-secondary education for the Wesley band. He gave me a paper of his entitled "The Plight of My People," in which he compared the dysfunction, alcoholism and violence of his community to that of Ireland and attributed both to colonization and abuse by a dominant foreign culture.

Greg's paper had a huge effect on me. I found the comparison with the Irish to be accurate. Even though my father drank only very occasionally, and my mother not at all, we had been close to other Irish families in which there were serious problems with alcohol and violence. Greg's perception gave me a sense of shared culture and history, and contributed to my compassion and concern for his people and the members of his community who appear in my court.

I made some comment about Ernest being responsible for the deficit, and he told me that was a lie, that there was no deficit. He had left a surplus.

They told me about the SITE program. When he became chief in 1992 Ernest had ended a practice of mixing education funds in with general tribal funds and had put a committee in charge of education, including funding for it. The school at Morley had been in chaos prior to 1992 and the new program and administration had made a huge difference.

Ernest said he wanted to talk about "world view" and I said I wanted to talk about justice programs. He said, "Justice? What's justice?"

I answered, "To me, justice on the Stoney Indian reserve would be every child having a safe, quiet place to sleep at night."

I don't know what it was that inspired me to say that, but it struck a chord with the women in the room. Belva admitted that they had grandchildren who did not have safe, quiet places to sleep at night and she wanted to support anything that would accomplish this.

It was Belva who used the expression "prison without bars" in referring to the reserve. This was an expression I used in my comments when I ordered the investigation of financial mismanagement and political corruption on the Stoney reserve in June of that year.

When I got up to leave, I mentioned that my father had been a friend of John Laurie. I said I knew Laurie was buried on the reserve and I wondered if they could tell me where. Belva told me he was buried in the Wesley cemetery located on the hill overlooking the old McDougall church. Then she seemed to tear up a bit and she said, "When you go there, look at the other grave markers. They will tell you a story."

Warren volunteered, "Oh yes, there is tremendous history up there."

Belva gave him a funny look, which I didn't understand at the time, but Warren seemed to catch her meaning and didn't say anything else.

It was a beautiful spring day, and on my way home I went to the cemetery. My usual route from Cochrane to Canmore is west along the 1A Highway toward the citadel-shaped mountain called the Devil's Thumb. In the winter it stands black among the snow-covered peaks, its sides too vertical for snow to accumulate. About halfway to Morley the road crosses the bridge over the Ghost River at its junction with the Bow. At that location the Ghost Dam holds back the waters that form Ghost Lake. The road continues between a campground on the lake side and boat storage and picnic tables on the other.

The campground had been the scene of a terrible accident a few years before, when a young Stoney lost control of his car as he rounded the curve above an area where a number of motorhomes were parked. He careened down the hill and crashed into two of the parked units, killing two of the occupants. He said he was afraid of the angry survivors and drove off. He drove about three kilometres farther west before his engine seized as a result of the accident. I recall the police paint on the road, marking the spot where the car had been abandoned. I excused myself from the case because I knew his family.

The car was abandoned right in front of Two Rivers Ranch, a place named for its location at the confluence of the Ghost and the Bow. The sign still says Stoney Medicine Lodge, but it hasn't been used as a treatment centre since 1996. Between the road and the river there is flat land where horses are often seen grazing, and grassy hills rise to the north. Another winding curve dips down onto a straight stretch where one can see the steeple of the historic McDougall church. The piece of road I like the least is a sharp dip through a little gully just before the old church. There are rails along both sides of the road at that point and the road is narrow. I often slow down to allow an oncoming vehicle to pass before I get there in order to avoid passing in the narrow gully, where there would be no way to avoid a vehicle that might cross the centre line.

There is a cross beside the road at the top of the gully that marks the location of a fatal accident.

Just past the church there is a road that goes north and up the hill to the cemetery. There is a cattle guard at the entrance. I parked my car outside and walked in. It was much different than the cemeteries I am used to. There were no monuments in straight lines, no neatly manicured lawns. It was a place that exuded sadness. The rough prairie grass followed the contours of uneven ground and grew around mounds of gravel where graves had been dug and refilled but no grass had grown back.

Many of the markers were just wooden crosses with the name and dates of the deceased painted on them. The ones that were a few years old were fading and some were almost impossible to read. I found the historic graves Warren Harbeck had spoken of. Andrew Sibbald, a teacher and carpenter, lies there along with schoolteachers who had worked at the residential school, and members of the McDougall family. I especially noted graves of young people. There were too many with birth dates after 1970. Some of the names I recognized; many of them were suicides. I thought of my own son born in 1970, and I thought of how unspeakable must be the sorrow of the parents of all of those young people.

I eventually found the place where Laurie is buried. His grave is covered with a granite slab and inscribed with the words:

In Loving Memory of Dr. John Laurie
He worked for the good of the Indians
And his white friends established the
Indian Association to help Indian
People with their problems. He was
A respected school teacher in Calgary
Ever remembered by his many friends
Both Indian and White

The plot is surrounded by a little fence and I had to bend down to read the inscription. When I straightened up, I saw the grave of Buffy Kaquitts. Her marker is a granite tombstone with her name and the figure of a barrel-racing rider etched into it. For some reason it was in that moment that the reality and the horror of the suffering that the Stoney people live with hit me. Perhaps her spirit spoke to me.

I broke down and wept. I cried out loud. I screamed at the Creator: "Why, why do You let this happen?!" "Why do these people suffer so much?" Then I thought: "Because nobody cares."

As I walked back to my car I noticed crocuses blooming. Their soft velvety petals decorated the rough, wiry prairie grass. My father would go out every spring looking for crocuses. I believe he was there with me and John Laurie and all of those young people who had died too soon. I thought that if people just knew what was happening, they would do something to change this. The Hunter case was outstanding and I thought all of this was relevant to his circumstances. I wondered how I could get all of what I was learning "on the record."

❖ 9 ❖

ROSE AUGER

After meeting Rose Auger at the Aboriginal Justice Learning Network, I became a regular visitor at her home. She would make tea from wild mint that she gathered along with other herbs. I liked that tea, and the conversations were always interesting. I asked her one time why she had come to Morley. She said it was because this was the worst reserve in the province and she wanted to do something to help.

Rose had a reputation as a medicine woman and healer, and many people would come to her for counselling and support. One day I dropped in and there were several Native women with her. We sat around the kitchen table drinking tea, and the conversation turned to domestic abuse.

I volunteered that I had never heard my father so much as raise his voice to my mother. The women sucked in their breath in shocked disbelief and then told me of their own experiences.

"My husband broke my arm."

"My husband put me in the hospital three times before I got away from him."

"My husband murdered one of my children."

I asked why it was so bad.

"Residential schools. We were abused in the schools and our parents were too. They never learned how to be parents, and neither did we. Now we have to start all over to learn about parenting and living together."

"Alcohol. We can't handle it but we keep drinking it."

"The reserves. No jobs. No self-respect. No respect for anything or anybody."

I asked if there was anything being done on the reserve in the way of programs that would help people deal with the dysfunction.

"Chief and council just look after themselves; the rest of us are on our own."

I thought about a night when I had been taken to the hospital in Canmore. I had had an accident while working in my garage and sustained an ugly cut that required stitches. While I was lying in the emergency ward an ambulance crew brought in a woman from Morley. They wheeled her into the emergency area on the ambulance gurney and then had to move her to a hospital bed. She was so badly hurt that she couldn't move herself. I heard the attendants and the nurses that were dealing with her.

"Careful, she has bruises all over, and we don't want to hurt her any more than she is."

They obviously moved her as gently as they could but she still groaned in pain.

Then I heard a nurse say to the patient, "Will you let us call the police this time?"

"Please, no. It will only make him more angry. It will just get worse."

I asked one of the ambulance attendants if they get many calls like this one.

"Too many. Between battered wives and attempted suicides we're back and forth all the time."

Rose Auger eventually convinced me to join her in a sweat lodge ceremony. Her son Cha Chee showed me the little dome-shaped lodge made of bent willow branches and covered with canvas. The entrance was only a few feet high and one had to kneel and crawl into the cave-like space. There was a pit in the middle of the floor where the hot rocks are placed to produce the heat.

Cha Chee was later charged with some serious offences and Rose wanted to talk to me about them and she wanted me to help him get into treatment.

"Rose, I'm sorry but I can't listen to you and then take this case and do what you ask. Our legal system requires that I be objective. I can't take cases where I know the accused or the family, because I would not be objective."

"Oh, that is so wrong. You make decisions that will affect a person's life forever and you can't even know those people?"

She let the matter go, but her words still ring in my ears. There was much truth in what she said.

In May of 1998 my chief judge would order me moved back to Calgary because, in his view, I had lost my objectivity with Aboriginal offenders. There is no question that my views in relation to Aboriginal offenders were changing dramatically. In my defence, I believe that what I had lost was my ignorance, an ignorance which had made it much easier to apply the law without much regard to the humanity, or rather inhumanity, involved.

There were six or eight of us who would participate in the sweat and we gathered in the living room of the house while Cha Chee stoked the huge bonfire that heated the rocks for the sweat lodge.

Greg Twoyoungmen's house, where Rose was living and where the lodge was located, looks south to the Goodstoney Rodeo arena and its grounds. In the distance one can see the hills on the far side of the Trans-Canada Highway. One of those hills has a huge ugly scar, the result of logging that had been done in many places on the reserve.

During 1996 an estimated $50-million worth of timber was taken from the reserve and shipped to mills in BC. Myrna Powderface was a plaintiff in an action to recover some of that money. While the majority of the people on the reserve lived in poverty, none of this money was ever paid to the tribal administration or made available for much-needed treatment programs.

In theory the whole reserve belongs to all of the people. The title to the reserve is in the name of the Crown in trust for the Stoney Indians. In theory, when these resources were sold off, the proceeds should have belonged to the people as a whole. In practice, even though there are no separate titles to the lands occupied by individual families, there is an accepted tradition that those lands belong to those families. What was happening with the timber was that individuals who claimed to own the timber plots were making private deals to sell their timber.

There were, of course, huge abuses. There were people brokering the sales – the brokers taking most of the money and some of the "landowners" receiving very little. I spoke to John Snow about this and asked why money was not available from the sale of timber for treatment programs. He told me there were people selling their timber "for a case of wine and a used car."

As chief, Ernest Wesley had commenced an action against Indian & Northern Affairs Canada and a number of the companies involved to stop the pillaging of the timber on the reserve. One of John Snow's first actions after being re-elected as chief was to discontinue the lawsuit. There was reasonably well-founded suspicion that he was benefiting from the logging and that the proceedings would have been an embarrassment to him.

As we looked out on those hills to the south, someone pointed out the clear-cut and referred to it as the "John Stevens clear-cut."

John Stevens, a medicine man, was credited with settling the Gustafsen Lake standoff in BC in 1995. He reportedly received millions of dollars for timber on his portion of the Stoney reserve. Some of the money was undoubtedly used to ensure the election of his daughter Philomene as chief of the Bearspaw and she no doubt supported John Snow in the discontinuance of the lawsuit.

After we had been chatting for a time, one of the men spoke to me.

"What do you do?"

"I'm the judge in Cochrane."

"Ohh, that's who you are. I quit drinkin' seven years ago and I haven't been to see you since."

This was Helmer Twoyoungmen. I didn't remember him from his drinking days, but I have seen him many times since. He has gained wisdom and virtue in his later years and has done a lot of work with youth on the reserve. It is men like Helmer who keep my hope alive for others who suffer from the disease of alcoholism. Others such as Ernest Hunter.

The sweat lodge was an amazing experience. Rose directed the placing of the hot rocks in the pit. We each crawled in and took our places around the pit. We knelt or sat cross-legged or in whatever position we could find in the very confined space. Cha Chee closed the flap over the entrance and we were immersed in total darkness. Rose invoked the Creator and the grandmothers and grandfathers. She sprinkled water on the rocks that quickly raised the temperature to something hotter than any sauna I had ever experienced.

We did the first round, in which each participant spoke of intentions and asked the support and help of the Creator and the spirits. At the end of the round we chanted "all my relations" and Cha Chee pulled back the flap and let in the daylight. We were able to crawl outside and cool down before re-entering for the next round. We repeated this for four rounds. The sincerity and intensity of emotion that I could feel in that hot, dark little space was far beyond anything I have ever experienced in any of the church services I have attended.

This was my first experience with Native spirituality at this level. We non-Aboriginal people often speak of Native spirituality as an Aboriginal virtue, but I believe we do this without knowing what it involves. This connection between the living and those who have "passed on" is a powerful part of it, but this is something that is little known to non-Aboriginals.

My own experience steeped in Irish Catholic mysticism – some will call it superstition – made this all very real to me. I believe my father and his old friend John Laurie were there with me in the sweat lodge and that they guided me in my actions and supported me in the aftermath.

❖ IO ❖

RUTH GORMAN

I often think of my father's comment that "God takes a hand in these things more than we know." I also embrace the Aboriginal spiritualism that includes the belief that the spirits of our loved ones watch over us and guide us.

One of my best friends was Lorne Jardine. We met at university and shared a room at the fraternity house. He graduated in medicine and became our family doctor. We shared many precious moments together, including the births of our children and the milestones in their growth. I am godfather to his daughter, Stephanie.

Lorne took his own life on the Ides of March 1992. His suicide is one of the most painful memories of my life. Perhaps the Creator wanted me to have that experience so that I might be more sensitive to the plight of those who lose loved ones in this horrible way.

In the spring of 1997 Stephanie graduated from nursing school. I attended her convocation on June 5 and joined her and members of her family for dinner afterward. In the course of the dinner conversation I talked about my efforts at Morley and mentioned my father's friendship with John Laurie. Stephanie became quite excited at my mention of John Laurie and said she had a friend, Christina, whose grandmother was writing a book about him and I should meet her. The grandmother was Ruth Gorman.

Ruth can be described as one of the first Indian rights activists. She was born in Calgary in 1914, obtained a BA in 1937 and an

LLB in 1939. She was only the second woman in the province of Alberta to become a lawyer.

Prior to the 1951 revisions to the Indian Act it had been unlawful for Indians to raise money to pay for lawyers, but lawyers could work for them pro bono. Ruth Gorman worked tirelessly for the Indian Association of Alberta and John Laurie. She described her relationship with Laurie as fellow soldiers fighting for a common cause. That common cause was the right of Aboriginal people to vote without being required to give up their treaty rights. Through her efforts, alongside those of Laurie and others, revisions were made to the Indian Act and the Elections Act in 1961 which allowed Aboriginal people to vote in federal elections without giving up their treaty rights.

After talking to Stephanie, I called Ruth. She invited me for tea. We became friends. Ruth had nothing good to say about John Snow. Her years of association with the Stoney people, and her credentials of being a real benefit to them, gave her comments about him significant credibility.

I think it was when I visited the Wesley cemetery that I formulated the idea of ordering an investigation of conditions on the reserve. I was satisfied I knew the answers to the questions I was going to ask, but I needed that information to be on the court record so that when I deviated from the legal precedents, the information would be there for the Court of Appeal to consider.

I told Ruth my intention. "I'm going to order an investigation of John Snow," I said.

"Don't do it," she replied. "He is an evil man and he will do everything in his power to hurt you."

We chatted for another while, finished our tea, and when I got up to go I said, "I want to thank you for your advice, but I'm not going to take it."

She smiled a little coyly and said, "I didn't think you would. Sometimes we just have to stand up and be counted."

That dear old woman, along with Tina Fox and Rose Auger and my wife, Laura, was a great source of strength to me in the difficult years that were to come. I thought I should write a book about them and call it *The Women Behind Me*. Ruth's book about Laurie was entitled *The Woman Behind the Man*.

In any event, Ruth was right about Snow doing everything in his power to hurt me, but that comes later.

Ruth Gorman died before she finished her book but it was completed by Frits Pannekoek and published by University of Calgary Press under the title *Behind the Man*. My name appears among the acknowledgements even though I had nothing to do with the production of the book. It was a beautiful "post mortem" tribute from a grand woman and steadfast ally.

❖ II ❖

THE INVESTIGATION

As I became more aware of the social conditions at Morley, and more concerned about them, the manner in which cases were prosecuted in Cochrane became a concern to me.

The Provincial Crown's office in Calgary conducted the prosecutions at Cochrane, and different members of the office came out on different days. It was apparent to me that none of the prosecutors knew very much about the Stoney community at Morley. I was trying to learn about it in order to overcome the criticism in the Cawsey Report about judges not knowing very much about the communities in which they work, and I thought the prosecutors should do the same. When I mentioned this to the Chief Crown Prosecutor at the time, Bruce Fraser, he said I was not the only one to ask this, but that his office worked better with the rotation system they were using.

I was overwhelmed by the social problems that were facing the accused people before me, and I was becoming frustrated at the lack of response I was getting from everyone I thought should be concerned about it.

When I made the order for the investigation of social conditions at Morley, I was simply thinking it would force the Crown to look at the situation, that it would perhaps motivate the chiefs to do something to save face, and that I would get a report that would put all this information on the record for the Court of Appeal. I would then write a judgment giving my interpretation of section 718.2(e) of the Criminal Code and it would be backed by the information contained in the report. My basic thesis was that if people looked at the abysmal social conditions in which offenders from the Stoney First Nations are brought up, and in which they live, they would have to realize that it is far better to help them than to just "throw them in jail."

In my career on the bench I had delivered very few written judgments. That was pretty much the wisdom of the day at the time I was appointed. The Provincial Court was the people's court and people came for quick dispositions, not for lengthy legal dissertations that they probably didn't understand anyway. I also disliked reading judgments. I found them to be boring, confusing restatements of the same principles, interspersed with hair-splitting distinctions that in my view often constituted a waste of time and resources.

My interest in Aboriginal justice changed this to a degree. I wanted to write something that would be a contribution to the development of the law in the area of Aboriginal justice. I therefore wrote out my thoughts, and on June 26 I read them into the record and adjourned Hunter's sentencing until the fall. [Please see Appendix A for the official text.]

On my way to Cochrane that morning, I picked up a hitchhiker. I had made a point of picking up hitchhikers ever since the case management meeting in which we discussed getting a bus to run from Morley to Cochrane on court days and I was told that this could be done if I would pay for it. I didn't realize who the hitchhiker was until he got into the car. It was Ernest Hunter. This would come back to haunt me later. As my friend Jeff Williams often says, "No good deed ever goes unpunished."

❖ 12 ❖

MEDIA COVERAGE

There is no question that I did not get the results from the investigation that I had hoped to get. However, I created a media stir that did accomplish my main objective. It exposed the abuses on the reserve that are a contributing factor to the criminal offences committed by residents and that therefore should be taken into account in determining sentences for those offences. This was, I believe, the proper application of the then new provision in the Criminal Code, section 718.2(*e*): "… with particular attention to the circumstances of Aboriginal offenders."

The day after I made the order for the investigation, June 27, 1997, there were articles in both the *Calgary Herald* and the *Calgary Sun*. The *Herald* quoted Chief John Snow as saying, "This judgment is just outrageous. It is inappropriate, false and racist." The article also said the tribal council had voted unanimously to file a complaint with the Judicial Council of Canada.

The next day, the *Sun* reported that the province had appealed my order.

I was experiencing a very tight feeling in my stomach which lasted for the next several years. I don't know how I survived the stress. Fortunately I had scheduled an extended holiday that summer and was able to leave Alberta shortly after making the order. My wife's parents live in Collingwood, Ontario. Laura and I took Carlyn, then 4, and Jamie, 2, and drove to Ontario, where I spent the summer splashing in the waves off Wasaga Beach and drafting the judgment I proposed to render in sentencing Ernest Hunter.

Meanwhile, back in Alberta, the newspapers were working hard to keep attention focused on the Stoney Indian reserve at Morley. The events of that summer were lamentable, but the deaths of six young Stoneys may have helped me keep my job. They certainly demonstrated that my concern for the social conditions at Morley were more than justified.

As a judge, it was not my job to seek the approval of the press. However, I had become the focal point of a very political situation, and favourable press coverage was to my advantage. It was a huge help to me in dealing with the stress of my situation and it made it much more difficult for my detractors to succeed against me. On June 28 the *Calgary Herald* reported the death of Patricia Bearspaw from liver failure "prompted by booze and prescription pills." The article went into detail about my order for the investigation and quoted people on both sides of the issue. Former chief Frank Powderface supported me. This was surprising to me because I didn't think Frank liked me. He was known for disliking white people generally. Greg Twoyoungmen supported me and said he wanted the truth to come out. Greg had been an opponent of Snow since the '70s and I gained a lifelong friend by my effort to expose Snow's corruption.

The June 28 *Calgary Sun* ran the headline "Ruling absurd" on an article picturing John Snow. It seemed the *Sun* was on the chief's side in this controversy, but the next day a column by Linda Slobodian was headed "Courageous judge upsets the applecart." I liked her article. It said, in part:

> So what did the province do? It moved swiftly. No, not to see if people are needlessly hurting. But to shut Reilly up. Justice Minister Jon Havelock said the province will apply to have Reilly's order quashed. Havelock said by ordering a probe of social conditions, alleged corruption and financial mismanagement, Reilly exceeded his jurisdiction. Then whose jurisdiction is it?

Many similar complaints have been made to the province, the feds and law enforcement officials by many people on different Alberta reserves. And still the government dollars flow in, and many reserves get huge oil and gas revenues, but housing is pitiful, in some cases water is unclean, and social problems, unemployment and crime are all high. Why is this? Reilly had the courage to ask. He's not alone.

On June 29 the *Herald* ran a great cartoon showing John Snow holding a newspaper with the headline "Judge Orders Probe of Band" and saying, "We didn't think white folks cared."

The next day, the *Sun* headlined "Indian Affairs Department Ripped." The story quoted Jack Ramsay, the Reform Party justice critic, confirming many of my concerns.

Also on June 30, the *Herald* announced "Stoney says natives afraid: Tina Fox." The story quoted Tina as saying, "People are afraid to speak out, there's a sense of helplessness. We are in a Catch-22. There are things going on in the community that people see are wrong but we have nowhere to go to make changes."

Fox also spoke about the resolution to file a complaint against me to the Judicial Council, and said that it was not unanimous as Snow had claimed. She was opposed but the vote had been called while she was in the washroom.

Tina also said that Snow had fired 39 people from the Wesley band and that the council had not been involved in those decisions.

On June 30 Jeffrey Perkins wrote an open letter to Justice Minister Havelock:

Re: The Stoney Indian Reserve at Morley
Sir:

In 1976 the American Indian Movement (AIM) undertook an armed occupation of the Morley administration offices. The issue was alleged corruption and financial mismanagement by the three chiefs and council.

Unfortunately, the "issue" was ignored: the presence of armed outsiders trying to tell the Stoneys what to do clouded the purpose of the occupation. Luckily the demonstration ended without injury or death.

The Stoneys who had asked AIM to come to their aid were treated badly. Those who were employed were summarily fired and told, in clear terms, that they would never get another job on the reserve. Others were castigated and derided by the chiefs at every opportunity; indeed, anyone who challenged the chiefs was treated this way.

Soon after the occupation, a (scheduled) election took place. The tribal administrator, Mrs. Tina Fox, was elected to the new council, the first woman to achieve that position. I was asked by the Stoneys to be their tribal administrator for three months. My tenure actually lasted about four years.

During the first two years I was able to establish financial controls and management systems which produced the first-ever unqualified audits for the Stoneys. During that two-year period there was an atmosphere of hope on the reserve. Suicides had plagued the Stoneys prior to the AIM occupation; now there was a sense of purpose, a feeling that the old ways of thievery, corruption and venality were past. Escape by suicide was not needed.

And then the chiefs returned to their old ways.

For example, the finance officer was ordered to deliver $30,000 in cash to a chief to be used as prize money at a powwow. No receipts were obtained and no records were submitted to the administration. It was reported that much of the money was paid to his family. This was not an infrequent occurrence.

Why allow this to go on? The administration was often asked this. The answer was simple: there is no law in place to stop it. The Indian Act demands no real accountability such as we expect and accept under the Alberta Municipal Act.

Money is given to families and clans to ensure their obedience. It is easy to do. The chiefs order that so and so be paid for a mile of fence. It is understood that no fence will be built! In fact, if all the fence ordered by the chiefs was actually built it would probably stretch from Morley to Ottawa!

The use of Stoney money to maintain power and to keep the Stoneys subservient was seen by the chiefs to be their Native right, and more importantly, they realized that no person or government organization, federal or provincial, would stop them. Any sign of concern was met with cries of "racism" and "paternal/colonial interference." It was also met with threats of legal action: no person could afford to go against the millions the chiefs had available for this purpose.

From the newspaper reports over the past few days it is obvious little has changed. Suicide seems to be the choice of young Stoneys who want to escape the corruptive pall which is destroying a people. The lack of moral leadership also engages the justice system in a never-ending replay of violence and drunken behaviour.

Wholesale firings of employees by chiefs for no cause have given rise to even more despair. There is no action that people can take. No one listens. The federal Department of Indian Affairs has one answer: it is your problem; you deal with it. But there is no way to deal with it. Except, perhaps, through Judge Reilly's approach.

Judge Reilly has done the Stoneys a great service, firstly in recognizing the underlying issues which bring so many

Stoneys before his court, and then by asking for an investigation. Many are hoping that at last something will be done.

Sadly, your initial reaction has caused that hope to be dashed. Once again, it seems, the political powers are giving explicit permission for the corruption to continue. Those responsible for the wrongdoing can now brag that they have the Alberta Minister of Justice on their side! I would urge you to reconsider your reported response. Do not attempt to quash the judge's request. Please encourage justice to be pursued in an open way.

I have stressed that there is no action the Stoneys can take, but unfortunately there is a frightening alternative which is not unthinkable given the level of frustration at Morley: violence, perhaps assassination.

Please, as the Minister of Justice, do not simply allow justice to be done, but help Judge Reilly and the Stoneys to work within the legal system to end the corruption at Morley.

At this time the Stoneys, as Albertans, need your help.

Respectfully yours,
Jeffrey Perkins

On July 1 the *Canmore Leader* headlined "Stoney chief says ruling a dangerous precedent." The story was an interview with Chief Snow in which he said that the order was a dangerous precedent for Native people across Canada. It also highlighted a quote from my order: "… the candidate with the most relatives wins and then he and his family share the spoils."

In the same issue of the *Canmore Leader*, a story titled "Thompson to visit reserve" quoted Myron Thompson, the MP for the riding of Wildrose, where Morley was located, as saying, "I think maybe the judge said some things that might be absolutely what was needed to be said and maybe we need to do some investigating."

On July 1 the *Calgary Herald* headlined "Feds to study call for reserve probe." The same issue ran a major story titled "Elder hopes call for change doesn't fall on deaf ears; but consultant says there is nothing new about judge's call for management probe." Evangeline Rider was pictured sitting in her wheelchair in front of her empty refrigerator.

On July 2 the *Sun*'s Linda Slobodian called me to give me a heads-up that a number of Native people were having a press conference and she was afraid they would say things very critical of me. This caused me some concern and I was pleasantly surprised when the next day the *Sun* ran an article headlined "Probe welcomed: Native bands say judge's order is only hope." The article had a picture of Hanson Twoyoungmen holding a sign that said "Stoneys divide and conquer." Linda's column, titled "People who matter push for change," cited comments from Roy Littlechief, former chief of the Siksika reserve, Bruce Starlight of the Tsuu T'ina, George and Blaise Good Dagger of the Blood reserve and Hanson Twoyoungmen of Morley.

The *Herald* also ran an article on the press conference, headlined "Residents of four reserves back judge's call for probe." Hanson Twoyoungmen was quoted as saying, "By allowing most funds to flow to a select few, Snow is helping to ensure most Stoney members are consigned to a life of poverty and substance abuse." Another article was headed "Chiefs express support – Reserve conditions primitive."

On the same day, however, Don Braid's column in the *Calgary Sun*, titled "Furore abounds in stereotypes," was sympathetic to John Snow, commenting on what a difficult job it is to be an Indian chief. I had in fact asked Snow, the day of our meeting in Cochrane, why he would want to be chief. He had no answer. I believe the answer of an altruistic statesman would have been automatic: "to help my people." I believe the truthful answer from him would have been: "because I can help myself to millions of dollars." I believe that is why he didn't answer at all. Braid's column did accomplish one thing, though. It suggested I should get a copy of the report of the Royal Commission on Aboriginal Peoples [see below at p. 137] and read it. I took that suggestion and read all seven volumes. It was a depressing part of a learning experience that was generally depressing.

Even the national paper *The Globe and Mail* reported on my efforts and the responses of Chief Snow and Minister Havelock: "Scandal cloud descends on Stoney reserve."

On July 4 the *Calgary Herald* headlined "Feds eye Stoney accounts: Federal Department of Indian Affairs looking at imposing financial management on the Stoney Indian Reserve because of their deficit reported at $4,000,000."

Two days later the *Herald* ran a full page headed "Stoney band's lost youth." It showed a picture of Frank Powderface holding a picture of his grandson Vernon Labelle, who had committed suicide by walking in front of a car on the highway. Frank was quoted as having said, "The devil is strong if you give up."

On July 8, under the headline "Klein queries judge's power," the *Herald* reported that Alberta's premier was taking the position that I had overstepped my authority and that the tribal governments would be dealt with on a government-to-government basis. Ralph Klein was doing exactly what Jeff Perkins had warned against. He was allowing those in power to brag that no one would stop them.

The same issue of the *Herald* contained an editorial headed "Hearing the judge: Native issues cannot be ignored."

In the July 8 *Calgary Sun*, Jack Tennant's column, headed "Time for premier to show courage," was an open letter to Ralph Klein asking him to look into the matters I had raised.

On July 12 *The Globe and Mail* ran an op-ed by University of

Calgary professors David Bercuson and Barry Cooper, "Seeking justice for troubled Stoney reserve." Their synopsis of the situation at Morley ended with this paragraph:

> Whatever the eventual outcome of this particular ruling, the significance of the lamentable business is clear: first, the Canadian criminal justice system has become incapable of dealing with the enormous problems that exist on native reserves. And second, the chiefs – and not just "Canadian society," the system or the Department of Indian Affairs – bear some responsibility for the terrible conditions, the unacceptable oppression and tyranny on the lands at least partly under their sway.

I agree with this comment about the criminal justice system being incapable of dealing with the enormous problems that exist on native reserves. That idea may form the basis of my next book.

On July 14 *Alberta Report* magazine's cover story was headed "Behind the buckskin curtain: An Alberta judge calls for an investigation into Chief John Snow's 'banana republic.'" The article spoke of 90 people being fired from their jobs after Snow's re-election, programs being cut and relatives of the chief being given jobs. The story mentioned that Chief Snow had excused himself five minutes into the interview for the article.

On July 16, under the headline "Stoney chief's power reined in," the *Herald* told of a resolution passed by the Stoney tribal council to limit the power of the chiefs. Previously the reserve's three chiefs could make decisions as an executive committee without consent from the council. The resolution gave each of the councillors an equal vote. The article said the councillors had not been consulted by the chiefs when about 100 employees, including 39 Wesley band staffers, were fired after the election held the previous December.

On July 19 the *Herald* reported that the opposition Alberta Liberals' native affairs critic, Sue Olsen, was urging federal Indian Affairs Minister Jane Stewart to launch an inquiry into the reserve: "Feds told to look into Stoney affair."

A July 28 piece in *Alberta Report* headlined "A Stoney silence: Judge Reilly's demand for a thorough inquiry into Indian reserve corruption seems doomed." The article seemed to me to be a fairly accurate summary. The provincial justice minister, Jon Havelock, was moving to have my order quashed. Indian Affairs flatly refused to investigate the allegations. Federal minister Jane Stewart was on vacation and could not be reached for comment. Stewart Swanson, the department's director of transfer payments, said there would be a few problems as native bands made the transition to self-government. Reform Party MP Mike Scott pointed out that the department had spent $2-billion over five years on Aboriginal job creation but unemployment on reserves had gone up, not down. The only bright spot was that the Stoney tribal council passed a resolution limiting the power of the chiefs in spite of John Snow's resistance. If I had something to do with that, then I can take great satisfaction from the fact that I had empowered the members of the Stoney council to do something for themselves.

On August 7 the *Calgary Herald* headlined "Minister not keen on Stoney inquiry." In her first comment since my order for an investigation the Minister of Indian Affairs said she did not wish to air dirty laundry by supporting the investigation.

Two days later, on August 9, the *Herald* headlined "Stoney death probed: Chief's niece fourth resident of reserve to die in six weeks." Carolyn Snow, a niece of Chief John Snow was found dead in the wreckage of a car that had gone over an embankment. The article mentioned that I had cited high numbers of alcohol-related deaths and suicide in my 12-page ruling calling for a probe into social conditions and allegations of financial mismanagement and political corruption on the reserve.

The following week, the *Herald* ran a story headlined "Reserve rocked by another death." Roland Ear, who had been involved in the crash that killed Carolyn Snow, had been found dead. The RCMP were said to be treating the death as suspicious – the rumour was that Ear had been beaten to death. Liberal MLA Sue Olsen called on the province to drop its challenge to my order for an investigation, but Justice Minister Havelock was still challenging my jurisdiction. Indian Affairs Minister Jane Stewart was still saying that airing dirty laundry was not in the best interests of the community.

The August 17 *Herald* carried the story "Brother charged: More calls for Stoney inquiry." Sterling Emerson Ear, 27, had been arrested and charged with second-degree murder in the death of his brother Roland Ear.

The next day's *Herald* headlined "Stoney affair federal case: Havelock." Opposition native affairs critic Olsen said the federal and provincial governments were passing the political hot potato while more people died. In my view, her description of the situation was accurate.

By this time I was beginning to find the news coverage somewhat amusing, but my heart wept for poor Indian people, who must get this "passing the buck" whenever they try to deal with problems on a reserve. I would think back to that day in the cemetery and I could better understand why all those young people were there. I had heard the answer "because no one cares," but I didn't understand it then the way I was beginning to understand it now.

The Assembly of First Nations had just elected Phil Fontaine as their new national chief, and an August 11 *Maclean's* magazine article titled "Fontaine's vision: The new grand chief aims for unity" made reference to the situation at Morley. It mentioned Vernon Labelle's death and pointed out that since the beginning of the year eight other reserve members between the ages of 19 and 26 had died. The story quoted my dear friend Bert Wildman, a Stoney elder, as saying, "A lot of the young people get frustrated – they think there is no tomorrow for them." It also quoted my judgment: "Fear, intimidation and violence appear to be a dominant part of life on this reserve."

Even BC was taking an interest in Morley. *British Columbia Report* that same week carried a story headlined "Just as hopeless as before, but governments continue to refuse to investigate the Stoneys." The article began: "It has been a month since Alberta Provincial Court Judge John Reilly ordered a Crown prosecutor to investigate conditions on the Stoney reserve, 37 miles [sic] west of Calgary. The only visible action taken is an application by Alberta Justice Minister Jon Havelock to have the order quashed. The death of a young man on the reserve two weeks ago prompted renewed calls for an investigation, but to no apparent avail." The article went on to talk about Stanley Rollinmud, the 21-year-old father of two who committed suicide by walking into traffic on the Trans-Canada Highway, the tenth young adult to die on the reserve that year and the third in a month. The story quoted Fred Jobin, the acting Alberta regional director for the federal Department of Indian Affairs & Northern Development, as saying, "Prior to Judge Reilly's declaration, the Stoney leadership had already recognized the problem and are working on dealing with it."

The August 15 *Calgary Herald* announced "Stoneys to tackle deficit." The deficit was now reported to be $5.2-million.

On August 17, in a story headlined "Brother charged: More calls for Stoney inquiry," the *Herald* reported that Sterling Emerson Ear had been charged with second degree murder in the death of Roland Ear. Jack Ramsay, the Reform Party's justice critic, was quoted as saying, "Judge John Reilly's request for an investigation, I think, is becoming more and more justified."

The August 17 *Herald* also reported, however, under the head "No probe despite murder charge," that Justice Minister Havelock had confirmed that his position had not changed.

In the *Herald* for the 19th, in an article headed "Human tragedy 'ignored,'" journalist Kim Lunman quoted Reform Party Aboriginal affairs critic Mike Scott as saying the situation at Morley was "a human tragedy and everyone can see that," and that "the government isn't living up to its responsibility." The story also quoted Rita Galloway, president of the Saskatchewan-based First Nations Accountability Coalition, who were planning a rally in Calgary: "We must not fail the judge. He's to be applauded. I wish there were more people taking a human concern for the Aboriginal peoples."

On August 20 a *Herald* story headed "Feds to act on deaths of Stoneys" began: "Federal officials are meeting with Stoney leaders this week to address social problems following a string of violent deaths on the reserve." My take on the article was that Fred Jobin, the regional director for Indian Affairs, was going to talk about it but wasn't going to do anything.

An August 21 *Herald* and Canadian Press story was headed "Havelock hikes pressure on feds for Stoney probe." Again this sounded good but it was just more buck-passing. Also in the *Herald* that same day was "Woman dies near reserve: sixth Stoney death." The article indicated that support for the investigation was growing.

Similarly, a *Herald* story from August 22, "Task force to probe troubled reserve," sounded hopeful, but it was just more talk about a proposal that as far as I know never materialized.

And on the same page of that day's *Herald* was "Latest victim counselled others." The story was about Abileen Dawn Hunter, who had completed a life skills training program and was working as a life skills coach until she was fired when John Snow was returned to office. This to me was one of the saddest stories. It would seem that Dawn had a chance to make a decent life for herself but losing her job was too much for her. She was lying on the highway when she was run over by a car. Readers can draw their own conclusion as to whether or not it was a suicide.

The August 22 *Herald* headlined, on page A2: "Fear and sorrow," an article quoting Tina Fox about her community.

On the 25th a *Herald* editorial was headed "Nobody's fools: Still waiting for a judicial inquiry into Stoney reserve affairs." This strongly worded piece said that the recent indications that the tribal government and Indian Affairs were dealing with the problems were not enough. The last paragraph read:

> The Stoney reserve is like a dysfunctional family desperately in need of intervention. We will not in good conscience turn our backs on our native neighbours.

This last comment, to me, is a complete answer to former premier Klein's position that reserves should be dealt with as government to government. That position means we will not intervene and we will in fact be turning our backs on our Native neighbours.

The *Herald* front page for August 28 was headlined "Former Stoney chief backs call for probe," with a picture of Frank Kaquitts talking with Reform MP Myron Thompson. The story quoted Frank as saying, "He (Reilly) did what he thought was good and I think he's right."

The *Herald* for that same date, on page A2, read: "Stoneys to borrow millions from bank; Tribe to borrow in order to deal with $5.2-million deficit."

On August 30, again in the *Herald*, was the headline "Indian Affairs initiates audit." The story reported that Fred Jobin, the regional director for Indian Affairs, had announced an audit by an independent firm, and that the Stoney deficit was now $5.6-million. Jobin promised to "get to the bottom of where the money went."

In that same issue of the paper, under the title "Minister calls for calm on reserves," was a story reporting that allegations of missing funds, both at Morley and at another reserve, Hobbema, near Edmonton, were causing tension that was becoming a serious concern.

The September 1 issue of *Alberta Report* headlined "Six dead Indians are worth an inquiry: Indian Affairs finally agrees to investigate the Stoney reserve but to what end?"

The *Western Catholic Reporter* that same day ran an editorial titled "Justice on the Morley reserve." There were a couple of paragraphs in the piece that I found gratifying:

> But whatever the Court of Queen's Bench decides, Reilly has done a courageous and important deed. His unusual request has drawn widespread media attention to the ongoing problems on the Stoney reserve and has emboldened reserve residents to speak openly to the media.
>
> Reilly has tried to shake things up on the reserve previously. He set up a native justice committee, a victim assistance committee and a sentencing circle. They all flopped because reserve residents, fearing repercussions to themselves and their families, refused to participate. Victims of sexual abuse and domestic violence, it is reported, also refused to testify due to similar fears.

On September 3 the *Calgary Herald* headlined "Exclusive interview – Expose Stoney injustices, says Reilly." This was one of the scariest articles for me. The tight feeling in my stomach became much tighter. I appreciated the work Kim Lunman was doing on the paper's continuing coverage at Morley, and I did agree to talk to her, but I did not want to be seen to be giving interviews to the press. I was under a lot of scrutiny from my colleagues and the chief judge's office – more than I realized – and an interview two days before the appeal of my order was to be heard might have been seen as serious judicial misconduct. Fortunately nothing came of it and I was accurately quoted: "I think there's been a lot of injustice on the Stoney reserve for a long time and that it's been allowed to happen because it's been kept hidden…. I'm just hoping that this time it's going to keep going until something happens."

On page B2 of the *Herald* that same day, under the headline "Stoneys plan rally for judge," the paper reported that Stoney band members and elders were planning a rally outside the Calgary courthouse in support.

On September 6 the *Herald* headlined "Don't quash probe, native leaders warn." The story reported on the Queen's Bench hearing to set aside my order and included a picture of former chiefs Norman Yellowbird and Robert Hunter, in their chief's regalia, outside the courthouse with MP Myron Thompson and Greg Twoyoungmen. On the next page was an article headed "Leader says Reilly spoke from the heart," which quoted former Stoney chief Ernest Wesley as saying the province should be supporting me in proceeding with the investigation.

I have great admiration for what Ernest Wesley did during his tenure as chief from 1992–96. He established a number of good programs on the reserve. Unfortunately, when he was returned as chief in 2000 his main objective was to separate the three bands completely. I could not agree with this. I see the division of the bands as one of the major stumbling blocks to social reform. Our disagreement in this regard was irreconcilable.

Here is a list of headlines from the ensuing few days:

❖ September 7, *Calgary Herald*: "Stoney families hungry, some welfare cheques a week late."

❖ September 8, *Maclean's*: "A season of deaths, tragedy plagues a resource-rich Alberta reserve." More coverage about the ongoing difficulties at Morley.

❖ September 8, *Calgary Herald*: "Stoney reserve petition calls for probe." Greg Twoyoungmen, who organized the petition, was quoted as saying, "Things are getting worse and it's only a matter of time before violence breaks out."

❖ September 9, *Calgary Herald*: "Stoneys face crucial meeting." Chiefs and councillors from Morley were invited to a meeting with Norm Brennand, a Calgary-based Indian Affairs official, in relation to tribal finances.

❖ September 9, *Canmore Leader*: "Courthouse rally backs judge's call for reserve probe." This report from my hometown paper quoted Stoney resident Bernard Bearspaw: "The chiefs and councillors got it made and the rest of us have nothing."

❖ September 9, *Calgary Sun*: "Reform MP backs Stoney petition." Myron Thompson supported Greg Twoyoungmen's petition but it only got 35 signatures. Greg was quoted as saying this was because people were afraid to sign.

❖ September 10, *Calgary Herald*: "Ottawa restrains Stoneys: Outside manager takes control of reserve spending." The accounting firm of Coopers & Lybrand was appointed as third-party manager to oversee Stoney reserve.

Another article from September 10, in Calgary's *Fast Forward Weekly*, was headed "Judge puts system on trial; Brave stunt reveals Stoney reserve epidemic." *FFWD*'s Nick Devlin, in my view, made some great comments in his editorial. I quote in part:

> Something is terribly wrong on the Stoney reserve. Young Natives are dying. Violently, senselessly, drunkenly – at a pace that would instantly be branded an epidemic in the non-Native community.
>
> One man decided to do something about it. Tired of watching the endless trail of broken and damaged people from the Stoney reserve filing through his courtroom, Judge Reilly took a stand. Using new and untested sections of the Criminal Code aimed at making sentencing a more human and contextually sensitive process, he refused to pass sentence on a man convicted of domestic violence until the Crown completed a comprehensive review of conditions on the Stoney reserve, covering everything from obvious issues such as alcohol abuse to more politically charged questions such as where the band's oil millions have gone with so many of its people still living in Third World poverty.
>
> Judge Reilly's order was a brave and crazy political stunt. There is little chance that his order will hold up on appeal, but that's not the point. This man, this powerful white man who makes his living moving people from the scenic ghettos we quaintly call "reservations" to the even worse environment of prison, tried to do the right thing. By his actions, Judge Reilly recognized the accused before him as a person caught in a complex tangle of social ills and injustice and not just another drunk Indian who beat his wife. And he tried to make the "system" finally deliver something vaguely resembling justice to the Native community.

In the *Calgary Herald* for September 13, "Reserve corrupt, Cree charge" headed a story about allegations made by members of the Samson Cree reserve, near Wetaskiwin, Alberta, about conditions similar to the problems at Morley.

The same day, the *Herald* also reported, under the headline "RCMP probes Stoney affairs," that Indian Affairs had turned over some files to the police. Sheila Carr-Stewart, regional director in Alberta, was quoted as saying the forensic audit "will go back as far as needed."

The next day, September 14, the *Herald* headlined "Stoneys give data to police." Ms. Carr-Stewart was reported to have also passed information to the RCMP concerning allegations of financial mismanagement on the reserve. Andrew Bear Robe, a member of the Calgary Chamber of Commerce Aboriginal opportunities committee, was quoted as saying the majority of almost 700 Aboriginal governments in Canada handle their money wisely, and that the Reform Party should "just stay out of our affairs."

On the *Herald*'s front page for September 15, "Chief used public funds for nanny" reported that Chief Philomene Stevens, leader of the Bearspaw, had used band funds to pay for a nanny for her children while a memo posted on an office door told band members there was no money for food vouchers or unauthorized medical needs. Chief Stevens was also said to have spent $18,000 on a week-long business trip to Phoenix, taking along a sister and two first cousins who did not hold elected positions with the band.

On September 15 *Alberta Report* ran an article titled "Bands on the run: Indians all over take direct action against their corrupt leaders." Among other things, the article said:

> At first it appeared little would come of Provincial Court Judge John Reilly's order for an investigation into physical and political squalor on the Stoney Indian reserve, 30 miles west of

Calgary.... But now it seems Judge Reilly's intervention has unleashed a maelstrom of activity: in the courts, in Ottawa – and especially in band offices, where frustrated Indians are taking matters into their own hands.

In the *Calgary Herald* for that same date, "Fontaine downplays Stoney financial woes" reported that the national chief of the Assembly of First Nations cast the Stoney reserve's financial troubles as normal problems experienced by all governments.

On September 20, the *Herald* headlined "Stoneys worried records vulnerable to tampering." Greg Twoyoungmen expressed the concern that moving Stoney records to an office in the Dome Tower in Calgary's TD Square would allow tampering therewith. Dave LaVallie, lawyer for the tribal administration disputed this.

The *Herald* front page for September 27 headlined "Judge upholds reserve probe," with a story reporting the main conclusions of Alberta Court of Queen's Bench Justice Sal LoVecchio's judgment of September 26. [See chapter 13.]

Page A3 of the *Herald* for that day headlined "Reaction to ruling mixed, Justice minister says decision on Stoney order backs government." Justice Minister Havelock was quoted as saying: "Quite clearly the Court of Queen's Bench has indicated that Judge John Reilly exceeded his authority.... This simply confirms our position the courts should not nor do they have the authority to order these types of investigations by government."

Hunter's defence counsel, Jim Ogle, however, said the entire case "is sending the strongest message possible about conditions on the Stoney reserve and it's time government listens." Ogle further noted that Justice LoVecchio had "upheld the bulk of the order of Judge Reilly. An investigation has been directed to go ahead. The issue is how far reaching it is."

On September 30 the *Canmore Leader* headlined "Ruling confirms interpretation, Reilly says; Judge hopes case leads to 'positive changes' on Morley reserve." The hometown paper reported the situation in a light favourable to me. An editorial, "Legal wrangling aside, Stoneys need real change in their lives," concluded with this paragraph:

> Judge Reilly also said he hopes the attention being focused on the Stoneys' plight will result in real on-the-ground change. We can only concur with that sentiment. We hope the result of all the Morley-related matters being looked into – including an audit of the tribe's books, a probe into misuse of funds at the Stoney social services office, and a case involving sexual abuse of youths at the Stoney adolescent treatment centre – is that ordinary Stoneys will lead fuller, more productive lives in the future.

In the October 10 *Calgary Herald*, "Stoney workers told to keep mum" reported that a memo issued at Morley warned employees not to give information to the media. Tina Fox said this was a scare tactic, while Greg Twoyoungmen's reaction was that the administration didn't want to look bad but they were looking bad.

The October 19 *Sun* headlined "Minister raps political judge. They clash over time-limit posts." Justice Minister Havelock had suggested ten-year appointments for judges. I was asked for comment and said it might conflict with the principle of judicial independence. The minister did not like my comment.

The *Herald* for October 22 headlined "Tribal courts mulled for area natives." The story reported that the province was considering setting up a separate tribal court system for Calgary-area Indians, but that Minister Havelock had said Alberta's decision to float the tribal court idea was not influenced by Judge Reilly.

On October 23, under the headline "Havelock considers limited terms for judges – 'Public faith lost,'" the *Sun* ran another article about the Alberta Justice Minister considering appointing judges to non-renewable limited terms "because of the public lack of faith in judges and the legal system." Again I was quoted as saying that Havelock might have to consider a Supreme Court of Canada ruling on judicial independence. I said it seemed to me that non-renewable terms would allow politicians more control over judges. Havelock had referred to lenient sentences, and I was quoted as saying, "The public's desire for tougher penalties is generally misplaced. Much of the problem is a lack of understanding."

On October 21 the *Herald*'s front page announced: "Stoney welfare probe widens – Social services manager faces discipline." The story reported that documents showed Shirley Poucette had received $66,000 in welfare and wages between December 1996 and September 1997. The *Herald*'s page A2 the same day headlined "Stoneys: Two-thirds of the population rely on welfare," saying that some Stoneys were living on as little as $200 a month in welfare. Poucette had said in a telephone interview with the *Herald* the previous week that the paper had no right to look into her income. Fired in 1996 by the former chiefs, then rehired after the band election, Poucette had been one of Chief John Snow's campaign managers. Prior to being rehired in social services, Poucette was said to have been paid thousands of dollars a month to attend meetings, with travel expenses covered. In February she allegedly received more than $4,000 in addition to $1,505 in welfare. The documents further revealed that in May Poucette had collected $850 in welfare while being paid $2,720 in salary and an additional $2,611 in travel, meetings and honoraria.

On October 24, under the headline "Government spending: Natives need more cash, says bank," the *Herald* quoted John McCallum, chief economist for the Royal Bank, as saying, "The deplorable state of Canada's First Nations today can be seen as a shame to the country as a whole; the costs of doing nothing are high and rising." Phil Fontaine, the national chief of the

Assembly of First Nations, said scars of past abuse must heal before Aboriginals could move ahead. Indian Affairs Minister Jane Stewart wouldn't offer an apology or solutions, saying only, "It's incumbent upon us to find ways to allow the healing to occur."

Bill Kaufmann's column in the *Calgary Sun* for October 27, titled "Fresh approach to justice," seemed to support me. He quoted me as saying, "Our system for too long has been throwing people away." "What we have is a penal system that doesn't seek to repair." "There is general agreement among the public the prison system doesn't work; then they turn around and say put them away longer." Kaufmann then wrote of my support of community justice forums and the advantages to be gained from developing understanding between perpetrators and victims. He concluded with his very best:

> With a consciousness coloured by convention, I find it difficult to have as much faith in non-traditional sentencing as Reilly.
>
> Even so, here's a judge willing to speak out and actively engineer alternatives and swim bravely against powerful societal currents.

On November 4 the *Herald* reported that the "Stoney audit will last until spring." At least my efforts to expose financial difficulties on the reserve had produced some control over the tribal chiefs.

The November 19 *Herald*, under the heading "Judge calls Stoney report a failure; Response from band criticized," took notice that the Crown prosecutors office's 14-page report basically contained some statistical information on assaults, domestic assaults, deaths and suicides. In the same issue of the paper, "The Stoney report" gave full-page coverage on a very disappointing result after five months of stressful anticipation and media attention.

On November 20, under the headline "Leaders denied response, says tribe official," the *Herald* quoted Rick Butler, the tribe's administrator, as saying the court-ordered investigation into the Stoney reserve denied its leaders a chance to fully respond. This was pretty ironic in view of the fact that they refused to respond. [See letter excerpt, p. 122.]

On page B2 of that day's *Herald* was the headline "Stoneys following through on audit, says administrator." Butler said the bands were balancing the budget, eliminating the $5.6-million deficit and maintaining essential services. Sue Olsen, justice critic for the Alberta Liberals, criticized Havelock for not working co-operatively. Havelock said his department answered the questions they were asked. Beryl Kootenay, a Stoney activist, said the province's "overnight" report and Indian Affairs' efforts on the reserve didn't address the need for a more extensive investigation. Greg Twoyoungmen said Indian Affairs was "hoping this thing blows over." Reform MP Myron Thompson was quoted as saying the plight of the Stoney people lies squarely on the shoulders of Indian Affairs. "They would like to sweep it under the carpet and carry on like they have for years and do nothing," he said. This was true then and appears to be true today.

On November 26 the *Herald* headlined "Leaked Indian Affairs report: Native welfare abuse rampant." The story reported that a 1996 Indian Affairs report revealed the department was spending $700-million a year on a social assistance system that was rife with double dipping. The report further indicated that problems with First Nations welfare funding were nationwide. The story quoted Reform Party Indian Affairs critic Mike Scott as saying the human cost was a situation like the Stoney reserve, "where you have $15,000 in revenue for every man, woman and child on that reserve and yet people are living in appalling conditions." The story reiterated that eight Stoneys had died violently since Judge Reilly raised concerns of corruption on the reserve.

On November 29 the *Herald* ran a story titled "Stoney problem blamed on elite: Judge Reilly says province, feds fuelled frustration on reserve." On November 28 I had filed my written reasons for judgment in the Hunter case and Kim Lunman and Bob Beaty had taken excerpts from it.

The November 30 *Herald*, under the headline "Judge's removal predicted," reported that University of Calgary law professor Chris Levy had told reporters he had heard I would likely be moved back to Calgary. Professor Levy often visited with the assistant chief judge, Brian Stevenson, and I later had cause to suspect that his comment to the press was based on one of those conversations.

On December 6 *The Globe and Mail* ran an op-ed titled "Some teen fatalities matter less," in which University of Calgary professors David Bercuson and Barry Cooper noted the public outpouring of grief over the deaths of six Calgary teens killed in a BC avalanche, Lisa Salter stabbed in Edmonton and Reena Virk beaten to death in Vancouver, while almost no notice had been taken of the 13 young people from the Stoney reserve who were murder victims, suicides or died in alcohol-related car accidents. They spoke of my efforts, for which I had been "condemned by reserve leaders, praised by reserve reformers and shunned by both provincial and federal governments." The last paragraphs read:

> Now there are rumours that he will shortly be removed from his courthouse near the reserve and assigned to Calgary.
>
> The conclusion is obvious: bureaucratic and political formalities matter more than the prevention of the needless death of young natives.
>
> A second conclusion is equally plain: the deaths of some young people in this country matter much less than the deaths of others.

I wept when I read their conclusion. It is just ever so true.

On December 14 *Cochrane This Week* headlined "Reilly 'safe for the moment.'" In an interview, Chief Judge Wachowich indicated there were no plans to move me at that time. The last paragraph read: "Asked if such moves might be made for political reasons, Wachowich said, 'You're asking me something I am not prepared to comment on.'" (This will be the subject of my next book. On April 4, 1998, he made the decision to move me to Calgary. He informed me of the decision on May 28, 1998, and I was to move as of September 1, 1998.)

The December 24 *Calgary Herald* contained a story titled "Stoney chiefs received $450,000." A confidential report to Indian Affairs disclosed that total tax-free incomes and allowances of more than $450,000 had been paid to the Stoney reserve's three chiefs, while Christmas cheques of $100–$200 normally distributed to each of the reserve's 3,300 members had been cancelled due to the deficit. Chief Philomene Stevens was quoted as saying no one on the reserve was going hungry: "They still get $30 every two weeks" in oil and gas royalties.

On page A3 that same day: "Chief's income includes salary, honorariums and perks." Another article in the same issue was headed "Stoney reserve: No blame placed by Indian Affairs." The story reported that long-time social-service employees had sent a letter to Indian Affairs on January 27 informing of abuses in the social services department but the letter was not forwarded to the RCMP until eight months later. In the meantime the department had racked up losses totalling at least $500,000 which formed part of the reserve's deficit of $5.6-million.

On December 27 the *Herald* headlined "The Stoney saga: Band mourns lost generation," a six-page article setting out the results of the exhaustive investigation the paper had conducted following my order for the inquiry the previous June. The authors, Kim Lunman, Mark Lowey and Bob Beaty, did a tremendous job.

They did what the governments of Alberta and Canada should have done.

Finally, the December 31 *Herald*, under the title "Calgary, 1997: The year in review," reminded readers of how the whole matter had begun: "June 26: Judge John Reilly postpones sentencing in a wife-beating case, saying he first wants a probe of conditions on the Stoney reserve. Chief John Snow decries the move, and the province later moves to appeal Reilly's order for an investigation."

❖ 13 ❖

THE HUNTER CASE CONTINUES

The government's appeal from my order for the investigation in
R. v. Hunter was heard in the Alberta Court of Queen's Bench by
Mr. Justice Sal LoVecchio on September 26, 1997.

I met Justice LoVecchio for the first time about a year afterward and found him to be a very personable individual. I immediately liked him, partly because in my mind I owed him for the
fact that I was still a judge. I believe he would have felt tremendous pressure to just allow the appeal and dismiss my order. I
hadn't anticipated the media interest that I was going to generate
when I made the order. By the time Justice LoVecchio was hearing the appeal, the media circus was in full swing.

He gave a judgment that was a brilliant compromise. He confirmed that I had the jurisdiction to order the investigation into
matters that were germane to the case before me. Had he not
done this, I don't think I could have done anything other than
resign. He went on to say that there must be some logical nexus
between what is being ordered to be produced and the matter
under consideration. He said in part:

> Judge Reilly wanted certain matters investigated for the pur-
> poses of the sentencing hearing. As I concluded earlier, he
> has the authority to do this provided what he orders has some
> logical nexus or relevance to the matter under consideration.
> Is the collectivity of what Judge Reilly ordered justified on the
> basis that it is all information he requires to make a judgment
> on imprisonment or an alternative sanction for Mr. Hunter?

With respect for the clear and well-founded intentions of Judge Reilly, the answer is no. Some of what he has ordered meets the patently unreasonable test for *certiorari* relief. I say this having regard to the admonition I gave myself that all due deference should be paid to the judge on the firing line, and that I should not substitute my judgment for his simply because I might not have requested the information he requested.

Justice LoVecchio then gave as an example that violence at the school was not relevant because Mr. Hunter was 42 years old, had not attended school for some time, had no desire to go to school and didn't live anywhere near a school.

My questions (7) to (12) [see Appendix A at pp. 210, 211], as to financial mismanagement on the reserve, he addressed this way:

Questions (7) to (12) are the most troublesome in the equation. Not because it is difficult to reach a decision on their relevance. That part is easy. They only in a very tangential fashion get at the real question. That question is the level of commitment in the community for a support network to provide assistance to the residents who have problems of the type this case is all about – namely domestic abuse and alcohol addiction. To get at this question by accusing some members of the community of essentially criminal conduct is inappropriate. Those individuals were not before the court on any charges and they, like all citizens, are entitled to due process. As I said earlier, it may be that problems exist in this area in the community. If that is so, the responsibility falls to others to investigate and, if appropriate, file charges. This is not the function of a court.

Objectively speaking, it was a good judgment. What he said was correct in law, and in grey areas where he could have gone either way, he supported what I had done. Subjectively speaking, he missed the point altogether. The proposition I wanted to advance, as a relevant circumstance of this Aboriginal offender, was that he came from a community that was dysfunctional from top to bottom, and that to punish him for being dysfunctional wasn't fair.

My information about the school was that there was a substantial problem with violence, that there was huge absenteeism because the problem of bullying was so bad that a significant portion of the student population was afraid to come to school. I wanted that information on the record because it was an example of how pervasive violence is in this community.

I was satisfied that the information I had about John Snow using his position to have a private school bus take his children to off-reserve schools was true. I wanted that in the report so I could use it as an example of the abuse of tribal funds and as part of the reason why there were no programs in the community to support people with domestic abuse issues and alcoholism.

Justice LoVecchio quite correctly said that the presence of community support for the accused would be a factor in granting him a non-custodial conditional sentence. The lack of such support would go against such a sentence. The point I wanted to make was that there was such a complete lack of these programs in the community and such a complete lack of support that it was understandable that Hunter had succumbed to the alcohol and violence and that it would be unfair and unproductive to just send him to jail.

So what did I expect? I expected a report that would tell the truth – a report that would describe the corruption in tribal government and confirm that there were no programs available on the reserve to deal with the dysfunction from which Ernest Hunter suffered, and that the reason there were no such programs was that the tribal elite took all the money for themselves and didn't give a damn about the people who needed those programs.

The report, as reduced by Justice LoVecchio's order, was produced by Alberta Justice on November 14, 1997. In relation to the questions I asked on domestic assault I got the following answers:

- ❖ there had been 59 reported spousal assaults in a two-year period (there were probably several hundred that occurred);

- ❖ 42 had resulted in charges;

- ❖ of the 42 complaints where charges were laid, four had resulted in guilty pleas and one in a peace bond; trials and preliminaries were set in 37, of which 21 were still outstanding;

- ❖ of four trials, three accused were found not guilty and one was convicted;

- ❖ of nine cases in dead files, four had been withdrawn because they had been consolidated with other matters, and five had been withdrawn due to lack of witnesses.

I had expected the statistics would indicate a very high percentage of cases of domestic assault that did not proceed because of lack of witnesses. It had been my observation that practically all the cases that were coming before me were collapsing because of lack of witnesses. It is my suspicion that witnesses are often intimidated by offenders or their families and that it is not a coincidence that those cases do not proceed. I thought it was to Hunter's credit that he evidently had not intimidated Rondi Lefthand.

Question 13 was three questions: "How many people have been terminated from their employment? What reasons have been given? What are the qualifications of the replacements?"

The report said: "Alberta Justice has requested this information from the Stoney tribal council representing the Stoney Nation.

The council has refused to provide this information for the reasons set out in their letter of November 13, 1997, a copy of which is appended to this report." The letter read in part:

> Further to your request for information with respect to the employment situation on the Stoney Nation, we can only provide some general comments at this point. As the leaders of an independent nation, the Stoney tribal council does not recognize the authority of a Provincial Court judge to order an investigation into matters on the Stoney Nation.

I found it somewhat amusing that on October 6, 1999, the Stoney tribal administration filed a complaint about my report in the Sherman Labelle fatality inquiry in which they said, in part:

> The evidence to which Judge Reilly refers in his report does not provide a sufficient basis for his findings about the Stoney Nation and its governance. He condemns the tribal government without having heard from its leaders and members. This contravenes the most basic principles of fundamental justice.

As to question 14, Cochrane RCMP confirmed that four officers trained to be the Stoney tribal police were not employed due to lack of funding.

In response to question 16, as to the incidence of drug and alcohol addiction on the reserve, Cochrane RCMP supplied the following:

> There were 2,858 prisoners in Cochrane from October 1, 1995, to September 27, 1997. Sixty-five per cent of these prisoners come from Morley. Seventy-six per cent of these prisoners were arrested for intoxication with no charges. Clearly alcohol is a problem on the Stoney reserve.

To question 17, as to the incidence of suicide:

> The Cochrane RCMP have identified a number of unnatural deaths on the Morley reserve and adjacent highways. There were 25 deaths from October 1, 1995, to September 30, 1997. In three of the investigations, non-Morley residents were the victims of Morley drivers who were charged with alcohol-related offences.
>
> Three of the investigations identified suicide as the cause of death. The Cochrane RCMP suspect that one of their other investigations was a suicide while four other investigations involving drug/alcohol consumption may have been suicide.
>
> All of the unnatural deaths reported by Cochrane RCMP involved drugs or alcohol abuse.

In response to the second part of question 17, as to what was being done about the incidence of suicide, Health Canada reported that a task force had been set up in August 1997 to review the situation. In other words, it seemed to me, nothing was being done prior to my order.

Since Alberta Justice's report in response to my order in *R. v. Hunter* did not deal with questions of political corruption and financial mismanagement, I filed a number of pages of newspaper reports, mostly from the *Calgary Herald*, setting out the information that the investigative reporters had made available to me. My fellow judges cringed at what I had done. A judge must use certified legal reports in coming to a learned judicial decision. Quoting newspapers was an embarrassment. As a matter of fact, the chief judge, in a critical letter, said my judgments in Aboriginal cases, including *Hunter*, were an embarrassment to the court.

Instead of 18 months in prison, which I knew was the appropriate sentence, I had sentenced Hunter to two years of probation, with terms that he take treatment and do community service. As I wrote that judgment, I could feel I had lost the battle, but I firmly believed that what I was saying, needed to be said. [The text of the judgment in *R. v. Hunter* appears as Appendix B.]

The Crown appealed. I can just imagine the judges of the Court of Appeal shaking their heads and agreeing that Reilly had been on the reserve for far too long.

In a judgment dated May 8, 1998, the court overruled my decision and sentenced Hunter to 18 months imprisonment. In giving its judgment the court referred to its decision in *R. v. Brady* (January 1998). In that case the court said that the new provisions in the Criminal Code "codify but do not change the law." My view is that Parliament had tried to change the law in relation to sentencing. The Alberta Court of Appeal basically said it was just business as usual.

On April 26, 1999, the Supreme Court of Canada decided the case of *R. v. Gladue*, in which it dealt specifically with the interpretation of section 718.2(*e*) of the Code. Here are some of the things the court said:

[33] In our view, s. 718.2(*e*) is more than just a reaffirmation of existing sentencing principles. The remedial component of the provision consists not only in the fact that it codifies a principle of sentencing, but, far more importantly, in its direction to sentencing judges to undertake the process of sentencing of aboriginal offenders differently, in order to endeavour to achieve a truly fit and proper sentence in the particular case....

[34] In his submissions before this court, counsel for the appellant expressed fear that s. 718.2(*e*) might come to be interpreted and applied in a manner that would have no real effect upon the day-to-day practice of sentencing aboriginal offenders in Canada. In light of the tragic history of the

treatment of aboriginal peoples within the Canadian criminal justice system, we do not consider this fear to be unreasonable. In our view, s. 718.2(e) creates a judicial duty to give its remedial purpose real force.

[48] ... The proposed enactment was directed, in particular, at reducing the use of prison as a sanction, at expanding the use of restorative justice principles in sentencing, and at engaging in both of these objectives with a sensitivity to aboriginal community justice initiatives when sentencing aboriginal offenders.

[61] Not surprisingly, the excessive imprisonment of aboriginal people is only the tip of the iceberg insofar as the estrangement of the aboriginal peoples from the Canadian criminal justice system is concerned. Aboriginal people are overrepresented in almost all aspects of the system. As this court recently noted in *R. v. Williams*, [1998] 1 SCR 1128 at §58, there is widespread bias against aboriginal people within Canada, and "[t]here is evidence that this widespread racism has translated into systemic discrimination in the criminal justice system."

[62] Statements regarding the extent and severity of this problem are disturbingly common. In *Bridging the Cultural Divide*, at p. 309, the Royal Commission on Aboriginal Peoples listed as its "Major Findings and Conclusions" the following striking yet representative statement:

> The Canadian criminal justice system has failed the
> Aboriginal peoples of Canada ... The principal reason
> for this crushing failure is the fundamentally different
> world views of Aboriginal and non-Aboriginal people
> with respect to such elemental issues as the substantive
> content of justice and the process of achieving justice.

[64] These findings cry out for recognition of the magnitude and gravity of the problem, and for responses to alleviate it. The figures are stark and reflect what may fairly be termed a crisis in the Canadian criminal justice system. The drastic overrepresentation of aboriginal peoples within both the Canadian prison population and the criminal justice system reveals a sad and pressing social problem....

I had put several years of diligent study into the judgment I wrote in *Hunter*, and the Alberta Court of Appeal simply commented that I had overemphasized the Aboriginal aspect of the case. The court otherwise ignored all of my efforts. The comments of the Supreme Court of Canada were a tremendous comfort to me, and I wondered whether the Court of Appeal might have decided *Hunter* differently had *Gladue* been delivered before they made their decision.

The decision in the Baret Labelle case, which was after *Gladue*, indicated that the Alberta court was still taking the position that not much had changed. Unfortunately "the recognition of the magnitude and gravity of the problem" of which the Supreme Court of Canada spoke is yet to come.

❖ 14 ❖

BARET LABELLE

On May 16, 1997, Henry John Anderson and his wife Tan Nguyen spent the day fishing in the Ghost River wilderness area. They camped for the night at the Seebe Dam campground. That same day, Marty Ear and Sherman Labelle were drinking together. At some time in the early morning hours of the 17th they met up with Baret Labelle and decided they would go and "shake" some vehicles in the campground.

The Seebe site is land that was originally a part of the reserve but was taken back for the installation of the hydroelectric dam that is located there, and for the townsite of Seebe, which was built for the Calgary Power employees who maintained the facility.

Many of the Stoney people feel historic resentment about being restricted to the reserve when they were once able to roam the entire continent freely. They feel even more resentment that after being restricted to the reserve, they then had large parts of it taken back. The two main take-backs were the railway and later the original highway, then known as the Banff Coach Road and now designated as the 1A. The area of Seebe was yet another take-back. Ottawa made these arrangements with the Indian agent. The fact that Ottawa appointed the Indian agent and then negotiated with him to take back the land is an unfairness that has not escaped many Stoneys. The old people talk about how unfair it was, and the young people share the resentment.

It was with this background that Sherman and Baret began

their shaking of the camper where John Anderson and his wife were sleeping. The shaking included loud banging and Anderson came out and confronted them. Sherman told Anderson that he was a white man and that he was trespassing on Indian land. Anderson was in fact an Ojibway and told them so, but this did not satisfy them. Sherman struck Anderson and they began fighting. Baret had taken the handle of a socket wrench with him and threw it at Anderson.

Anderson sustained severe injuries. There was a question as to who did what. Anderson was unable to identify his assailants because of his injuries. Marty Ear was the prime mover in the matter, but he did not take an actual part in the beating, and then he made a deal to testify against Sherman and Baret and was not charged.

On June 29, 1999, Baret pleaded guilty to aggravated assault and I directed that the sentencing would be determined by a sentencing circle that I would conduct. The delay from the offence date of May 17, 1997, was due to the fact that Baret had originally elected to be tried in the Court of Queen's Bench and the preliminary hearing had been delayed due to Mr. Anderson's injuries. Baret pleaded guilty following the preliminary hearing.

The sentencing circle was originally scheduled for September 7, 1999, but was adjourned to October 1 because Mr. Anderson was not able to attend. I arranged to hold the sentencing circle in the boardroom of the Provincial Building in Cochrane so that it could be done more informally than in the courtroom. I had attempted to have members of the community present and there were in fact elders there on September 7 who were not able to return on October 1.

At the conclusion of the sentencing circle I imposed a sentence of two years probation with terms. The Crown appealed and the Court of Appeal delivered a judgment disapproving of the form of my circle, my procedure and my result. The court did not, however, change the sentence.

The Court of Appeal said that my sentence was demonstrably unfit and that Baret should have gone to jail. But in view of his tragic circumstances, his age, his family obligations, his role in the offence, and most importantly that he had served the suspended sentence without a breach and had made some progress, the Court of Appeal was not prepared to revisit the sentence and impose a term of imprisonment.

My greatest disappointment in the appeal judgment was that it made no reference to the comments I made on the dysfunction of the community in relation to the ongoing problems of violence there. I say that we learn what we live and we live what we learn. The violence of this offence is a symptom of the community dysfunction. If nothing is done to correct that dysfunction, punishing offenders is not accomplishing anything.

I accept the comments of the Court of Appeal on the makeup of the sentencing circle, but in my view it was better to use the circle, imperfect as it was, than not use it at all. I have come to see that many members of this community see the justice system as an instrument of their oppression. The only way this perception can be changed is for the community to participate.

I believe there was huge benefit in having the participation of George and Sheila Labelle, who are acknowledged as elders in this community. The process allowed them to see a situation in which they were being asked for their input and they were being heard. I know that they appreciated my efforts personally. What I wanted them to see was that the justice system is prepared to listen to them.

In my view the most amazing part of the process, and one which I did not expect, was that the victim, Mr. Anderson, after initially asking for the accused to be imprisoned for one to two years, forgave him and asked that he be allowed to go free. This must have been a huge step forward in the healing process for him. While his physical injuries will remain with him for the rest of his life, his life may be far better because he has been able to let go of his bitterness. It is hugely disappointing to me that the Canadian criminal justice system so focuses on denunciation and deterrence that it cannot see the benefit of forgiveness and healing.

❖ 15 ❖

SHERMAN LABELLE

On the 21st of May 1998 Sherman Laron Labelle, aged 17, hanged himself on the reserve at Morley. His uncle, Conal Labelle, testified at the inquiry that Sherman had hugged him, told him he loved him, and then gone outside. Later Conal found Sherman hanging from a tree. There was a pail nearby which he had stood on, then kicked out from under himself after tying a belt around his neck.

The fatality inquiry into the death of this young Stoney gave me another cause to investigate and report on the horrendous social conditions at Morley.

The inquiry began on February 26, 1999. It could have been a very brief hearing. The Fatality Inquiries Act provides that when a death occurs in relation to a person in the care of the government there must be an inquiry. Sherman was the subject of a permanent guardianship order and therefore the inquiry was mandatory.

The procedure is for the Justice Department to appoint counsel, who determines the witnesses to be called and provides this list to the judge who will preside. The lawyer does this, but technically it is the judge who directs the witnesses to attend, and the judge has the power to direct any witness he believes has relevant information about the death. The judge must then produce a report which sets out the date, time, place, medical cause, manner and circumstances of the death.

If there is one word that will define my life as a judge it is "circumstances." In the Hunter case it was the Criminal Code direction to have "particular attention to the circumstances of Aboriginal offenders" that led me to the steps I took and the judgment I wrote. Now I was presiding at a hearing that again required me to set out "circumstances," in this case those of a young man's death. I hardly had to hear any evidence to know that the circumstances of a young Stoney suicide on the reserve at Morley would involve all of the dysfunction that permeates that community.

On the first day of the hearing, counsel called five witnesses: the boy's uncle, who was the last person to speak with him; the medics and the police who attended; and the program manager for Stoney Child & Family Services. These witnesses were sufficient to establish that Sherman was a troubled teen who had hanged himself, and that could have been the end of the story.

However, I was also required to make recommendations to prevent similar deaths. In my view the only proper way to make such recommendations was to deal with the much wider problem of Aboriginal suicides and the circumstances in which they were occurring.

I had been criticized in the Hunter case for relying on my own knowledge of the conditions at Morley. I'd been told I should have called witnesses to testify about these conditions. In *Hunter* I didn't feel I could justify further delays in sentencing by adjourning the matter, but now I was presiding at a hearing which had no such time constraints. I could take as long as I saw fit to deal with the issues. Accordingly, I directed the calling of further witnesses and adjourned the inquiry to June 1999.

The facts of the death were simple enough. Sherman hanged himself. His life was a sad commentary on the life of an Aboriginal child. The report would have been complete had I just set out his personal circumstances, confirmed that his death was a suicide, and concluded that, given the circumstances of his life, there were no recommendations I could make that would prevent similar deaths. I am confident that had I done this, there would have been no comment whatsoever from the tribal government. However, I was not content to just gloss over the death of another young Stoney.

The inquiry report briefly set out that Sherman Labelle was 17 years old, born on the Stoney Indian reserve at Morley, Alberta. His mother had died on May 21, 1994, but Sherman had already become a ward of the Director of Child Welfare shortly before that due to his mother's inability to care for him. He had been in 16 different foster-care placements in four years. He had also been in treatment programs at Morley and at the Selkirk Healing Centre in Manitoba but was said to be resistant to treatment.

On May 17, 1997, Sherman and two other young Stoneys allegedly assaulted Henry John Anderson and left him permanently crippled. Sherman was to go to trial on June 10, 1998, on charges of aggravated assault. The anxiety of going to court undoubtedly contributed to the distress that led him to kill himself. On the night he hanged himself he was drunk. His blood alcohol level was 220 mg in 100 ml of blood. [The Criminal Code threshold for impairment is 80 mg in 100 ml of blood, the number popularly known as ".08".]

As I have said, this would have been sufficient to complete my function as the presiding judge at the fatality inquiry, but I was determined to go further. I stated in my report that Sherman's community circumstances were also a relevant consideration. I outlined some of the evidence to illustrate that Sherman Labelle's suicide was only one of a disproportionate number of suicides in his community.

Tina Fox was a Stoney tribal council member in her seventh term. She testified she had kept a diary from 1990 to 1998 which showed 120 drug- and alcohol-related deaths and 48 by suicide. In a community of 3,000, 48 deaths in eight years, or an average of six per year, is an annual rate of 20 per 10,000 population, which is ten times the national average of 2 per 10,000.

The same witness who said Sherman had been resistant to treatment agreed that the mental health and alcohol treatment programs were two of the weakest on the reserve.

A Stoney childcare worker who'd worked with Sherman said his file was disorganized and did not show respect for Sherman. She said he did not like white people telling him about healing, that he needed support which he did not get, that when he was in the Selkirk Treatment Centre in Manitoba he went AWOL and called her, saying he was really lonely. She said that in the five years she was with Stoney Child & Family Services she did not get training she asked for, and she felt that proper training was not as available to Stoney childcare workers as it was to others in the province. She also said she was among five workers that were let go due to chief and council.

Sherman was in need of appropriate care, but the Stoney Adolescent Treatment Ranch, a facility for the treatment of teenage alcoholism at Morley, had been closed two years before because of allegations of sexual abuse by staff. They were trying to reopen it but would lose their funding if this were not done by October 1, 1999. As it turned out, the facility has never reopened.

Sherman was also said to have been having difficulties in school, and home schooling had been arranged for him because of absenteeism. This led me to ask for further information about the school.

D'Arcy Dixon, the Bearspaw chief who was on the reserve's education committee, was the first witness when the inquiry resumed. He talked about how the school should have an environment of learning and should involve the parents, but he admitted that the facilities at the Morley school were limited and that he was sending all three of his own children to off-reserve schools. This in my view was typical of the disregard that some leaders have for their own people on Indian reserves.

The newly appointed superintendent of schools for the Stoney Nation, Gerry Brown, said he was excited about the prospects for the future of the school. He spoke of reopening industrial arts, home economics, music, and he said the computer situation was desperate. He said these programs had been discontinued three years before because of funding cutbacks, but indicated there were many more people on the payroll than necessary. He also said that the last students to have graduated from the Morley school had done so 10 to 12 years previously.

Former members of the Nakoda Education Management Team (NEMT) testified there had been a successful education program from 1992 to 1996 which had in fact produced two graduates in 1993/94, six in 1994/95, and seven in 1995/96. I believe that the testimony of the current superintendent may have been inaccurate because of selective information given to him by the current administration.

Witnesses spoke of the other successes the NEMT had had in leadership and life skills programs, and a former principal of the high school at Morley said she believed Sherman Labelle would still be alive if he had been able to take the leadership program created by NEMT.

NEMT and its programs were summarily abolished after the election of December 1996. The reason given by the new tribal council was a lack of funding. The former director of adult and post-secondary education said she believed this explanation was a lie, that the funding had been obtained through INAC (Indian & Northern Affairs Canada), HRDC (Human Resources Development Canada) and WOP (Work Opportunities Program) and that the new council had simply refused to sign the applications. She suggested, and this was supported by other witnesses, that the real reason the programs had been discontinued was to prevent the advancement of Stoney people so that they could be controlled by those in power.

Greg Twoyoungmen, a member of the tribal council, spoke of a proposed business development plan that was opposed by one man (a chief) because he did not want to allow the opportunities for employment that it would create. He testified at length as to the repression of Stoney people as a form of control, and said that tribal income is spent on social services instead of economic development, as part of a deliberate policy of keeping people dependent so they can be controlled. He volunteered his theory that this control leads to the depression that leads in turn to suicide.

Having heard these witnesses, I found that the community circumstances which must be considered as part of the context of Sherman Labelle's death included the following:

1. a lack of adequate treatment programs for mental health and alcohol problems that might have helped him with his difficulties in these areas

2. a lack of trauma counselling that might have helped him deal with the loss of his mother when he was 14 years old

3. a school where jobs were given to family members of those in power, regardless of qualifications, and teachers and administrators were fired for political reasons, leaving chaos for the students

4. the conduct of a tribal government that appeared to be deliberately sabotaging education, health and welfare and economic development in order to keep the people uneducated, unwell and unemployed so that they could be dominated and controlled

I then drew on my own research to further expand my view of the circumstances of Canadian Aboriginal people generally that contributed to Sherman Labelle's death.

Olive Dickason, in her book *Canada's First Nations*, for example, says that the suicide rate among Natives is six times that of the nation as a whole, and makes the bold statement that for Aboriginals under age 25, it is the highest in the world.

The Royal Commission on Aboriginal Peoples (RCAP, 1991–1996) in "Choosing Life: Special Report on Suicides among Aboriginal Peoples," wrote:

> After extensive consultation and study, commissioners have concluded that high rates of suicide and self-injury among Aboriginal people are the result of a complex mix of social, cultural, economic and psychological dislocations that flow from the past into the present. The root causes of these dislocations lie in the history of colonial relations between Aboriginal peoples and the authorities and settlers that went on to establish "Canada," and the distortion of Aboriginal lives that resulted from that history.
>
> We have also concluded that suicide is one of a group of symptoms, ranging from truancy and law-breaking to alcohol and drug abuse and family violence, that are in large part interchangeable as expressions of the burden of loss, grief and anger experienced by Aboriginal people in Canadian society. (p. 4)
>
> The rate of suicide among Aboriginal people in Canada for all age groups is two to three times higher than the rate among non-Aboriginal people. Among Aboriginal youth aged 10 to 19 years, the suicide rate was five to six times higher than among their non-Aboriginal peers; however, it is in the years between 20 and 29 that both Aboriginal and non-Aboriginal people showed the highest rates of suicide. (p. 5)

As Sherman Labelle's death was part of a Canada-wide problem, I found it appropriate to consider the history of this problem and the present-day effects of that history.

The stated policy of every Canadian government, from before Confederation until the abandonment of a policy White Paper on the matter by a Liberal government in 1969, had been to assimilate the Aboriginal people. This meant absorbing them into the general population so completely that it would be as though they had never existed as a people.

> The first prime minister, Sir John A. Macdonald, soon informed Parliament that it would be Canada's goal "to do away with the tribal system and assimilate the Indian people in all respects with the inhabitants of the Dominion." (Report of the Royal Commission on Aboriginal Peoples, vol. 1, p. 179)

There are those who will say that this is history and the non-Aboriginal Canadians of today should not be responsible for the wrongs of our ancestors. To these people I say that we are still enjoying what our ancestors took from these people, and we should take responsibility for what they did to these people. We are responsible for what they suffer today if we continue to do nothing about it.

The policy method was to make life as an Indian so miserable that Indians would not want to be Indians. The policy theory was that Indians would want to leave their old ways and embrace the superior white culture. It was an expression of what by today's standards would be regarded as the worst of bigoted white racism. While the policy has been officially abandoned, I believe that the processes it set in motion are still working toward the destruction of Indian peoples as people.

The policy tools were treaties, Indian Act control, Indian reserves, Indian agents and residential schools. The process involved assuming complete control over the lives of Indians through the provisions of the Indian Act and the totalitarian power of Indian agents; confining the Indians on reserves until they were sufficiently "civilized" and educated to join mainstream society; and taking children from their families and placing them in residential schools which were designed to "take the Indian out of the Indian child" and transform them into white Christians.

While the policy was unsuccessful, the injury that was done to these people in terms of social, psychological and economic privation remains with them today.

When the treaties were signed, Indians were promised that their way of life would be preserved and they would be able to pursue their traditional ways of life. Treaty 7 was made with the Stoney, the tribes of the Blackfoot Confederacy and the Tsuu T'ina in 1877. At that time, the Indians were stronger than the few whites who were on the prairies. After the railway came to Alberta in 1883, however, extensive white settlement soon resulted in the whites outnumbering the Indians and they began the process of taking away the Indians' freedom and their way of life. In 1885 the spiritual practice called the sun dance was declared criminal, and a pass system was instituted whereby Indians could not leave reserves without permission from the Indian agent. Parents who did not allow their children to be taken to the residential schools could be charged criminally.

Reserves were intended as holding places where Indians would stay until they were sufficiently educated and Christianized to join "white" society. I believe that what the white people did not understand is the Aboriginal concept of community. Where the white people emphasize individuality and "making it on your own," the Aboriginal emphasis is on "relationship." The Indian people did not want to leave their communities and embrace white society, with the result that many have been left on reserves, which are just holding places where they have no purpose and no future.

The reserve Indians were controlled by the use of Indian agents. This colonial practice would involve obtaining the collaboration of one or two families to help control the rest. The co-operation of these families would be obtained by favouring them with extra rations and privileges. The Indian agent had virtually absolute power. He determined who received rations and who did not. A person could not run for chief without the agent's consent. The agent determined who could leave the reserve and who could not. He had the authority of a judge, so he could charge, hold a trial and punish. No complaints could be taken to Indian Affairs except through the Indian agent, so there was no recourse if an agent was unfair. During the Second World War, for example, the wives of Canadian soldiers received a spousal benefit, but in the case of Aboriginal soldiers, the spousal benefit was paid to the Indian agent. Some of them used it for the benefit of the spouse, and some of them did not. In the latter case, there was no remedy.

As the Royal Commission on Aboriginal Peoples pointed out:

> Under terms of the Gradual Enfranchisement Act of 1869 traditional Indian governments were replaced by elected chiefs and councillors and virtually all decisions required the approval of a federally appointed Indian agent and/or the minister responsible for Indian Affairs. (RCAP report, vol. 2, p. 785)

I believe that this extremely autocratic and unfair system of governance was the role model for the future elected chiefs. When the use of Indian agents was discontinued in the 1960s, the families that had been used to control the others were more powerful because of the favoured position they had enjoyed under the

Indian agents. Those who got their clan leader elected chief were able to continue the same colonial method of governance they had learned from the Indian agent style of governance.

Witnesses at the Labelle fatality inquiry spoke of the power-lessness of the people. One said reserve residents have power on one day only, election day, and then it is gone for another two years. Witnesses spoke of the damage done by "phony tribal custom." This, they explained, was the concept of Indian chiefs, which are not a part of their tradition at all. The Royal Commission heard much the same thing:

> Many First Nations interveners spoke of how the Indian Act system of government had eroded traditional systems of accountability, fostered divisions within their communities, and encouraged what amounted to popularity contests. The first past the post system, whereby the greatest number of votes elected a candidate, was seen as especially problematic. It permitted large families to gain control of the council and shut other families out of the decision-making process. (RCAP report, vol. 2, p. 133)

The RCAP report also discussed the effect this has on reserve residents' health:

> Commissioners have concluded that the lack of economic and political control that Aboriginal people continue to endure, both individually and collectively, contributes significantly to their ill health. (vol. 3, p. 218)

As for the residential schools, although those institutions were mostly phased out during the 1960s, the horror of them for the Indian people and their continuing effect cannot be overstated. The RCAP report describes many problems: cruelty, lack of proper nutrition and healthcare, poor education.

The removal of children from their homes and the denial of their identity through attacks on their language and spiritual beliefs were cruel. But these practices were compounded by the too frequent lack of basic care – the failure to provide adequate food, clothing, medical services and a healthy environment, and the failure to ensure that the children were safe from teachers and staff who abused them physically, sexually and emotionally. In educational terms too, the schools – day and residential – failed dramatically, with participation rates and grade achievement levels lagging far behind those for non-Aboriginal students. (vol. 1, p. 187)

Children were frequently beaten severely with whips, rods and fists, chained and shackled, bound hand and foot and locked in closets, basements and bathrooms, and had their heads shaved or hair closely cropped. (vol. 1, p. 369)

Badly built, poorly maintained and overcrowded, the schools had deplorable conditions which were a dreadful weight that pressed down on the thousands of children who attended them. For many of those children it proved to be a mortal weight. (vol. 1, p. 356)

Scott (Duncan C. Scott, Indian Affairs, 1867–1912) asserted that, system wide, "50 per cent of the children who passed through these schools did not live to benefit from the education which they had received therein." (vol. 1, p. 357)

The system failed to keep pace with advances in the general field of education, and because the schools were often in isolated locations and generally offered low salaries, the system had been unable to attract qualified staff ... as late as 1950, "over 40 per cent of the teaching staff had no professional training. Indeed some had not even graduated from high school." (vol. 1, p. 345)

> Although the department admitted in the 1970s that the cur-
> riculum had not been geared to the children's "sociological
> needs," it did little to rectify the situation. (vol. 1, p. 346)

The lingering effect of these schools is family dysfunction that comes from generations of Indian children being brought up in them and therefore not having the experience of being raised by their own parents and thus not learning the parenting skills they needed to raise children of their own.

Prior to my study of the Indian question it was my naïve view that the purpose of the Department of Indian Affairs was to support and help the Indian people. I am now inclined to believe that the opposite is the case.

There is no question that the department, in its various forms since Confederation, was created to implement Indian policy, and Indian policy was to contain the Indians until they were assimilated into the general population and no longer existed as distinct peoples. While the policy the department was implementing has officially changed, I believe the processes of paternalism, fostering dependency and discouraging development on reserves so that the people will move off of them, are still at work. The RCAP report put it this way:

> ... the Indian Act was intended to hasten the assimilation, civi-
> lization and eventual annihilation of Indian nations as distinct
> political, social and economic entities. It was not intended as
> a mechanism for embracing the Indian Nations as partners in
> Confederation or for fulfilling the responsibilities of the treaty
> relationship. Rather, it focused on containment and disem-
> powerment – not by accident or by ignorance, but as a matter
> of conscious and explicit policy. The breaking up of Aboriginal
> and treaty nations into smaller and smaller units was a delib-
> erate step toward assimilation of Aboriginal individuals into
> the larger society. (vol. 2, p. 89)

The policy of assimilation had its roots in the 19th century, when governments in Canada and the United States – motivated by both philanthropic ideals and notions of European cultural and racial superiority – tried through civilization and enfranchisement legislation to eliminate distinct Indian status and blend Indian lands into the general system. Thus imprinted on the corporate memory of the Indian Affairs department well into this century was the attitude that Indian people required protection because they were inferior – although with proper education and religious instruction they could be turned into productive members of society.

Such views became deeply rooted in Canadian society as a whole. As the Penner committee on Indian self-government observed in its 1983 report to Parliament, it is only since the mid-1970s that public perceptions have started to shift. Even today many Canadians subscribe to the goals elaborated by Walter Harris; they do not understand why one sector of Canadian society should have treaties with another. They continue to believe that the solution to land claims and other issues lies in Aboriginal peoples' integration and assimilation into mainstream society. Such views are being rejected explicitly, however, in emerging international legal principles, and assimilation policies have been criticized by major religious institutions. (vol. 2, p. 554)

Volume 2 of the RCAP report is titled "Restructuring the Relationship," and in it the commission confirms that the whole arrangement between the federal government and the Aboriginal peoples of Canada needs to be changed. The commission recommended that

the Government of Canada present legislation to abolish the Department of Indian Affairs & Northern Development and to replace it by two new departments: a Department of Aboriginal Relations and a Department of Indian & Inuit Services. (vol. 2, p. 373)

In my report on the Labelle fatality inquiry, after quoting these passages about the circumstances of Canadian Aboriginal people generally, I set out the following conclusions:

1. Sherman was a part of the complex mix of social, cultural, economic and psychological dislocations that are the result of the history of Indian policy in Canada.

2. He suffered the burden of loss, grief and anger experienced by Aboriginal people in Canadian society.

3. His reserve was a place of helplessness and hopelessness that he was unable to leave because of a history of dependence that was imposed on his people.

4. His tribal government was the natural result of the history of colonial relations and colonial control of Aboriginal peoples.

5. His lack of family support was a part of the damage done by the residential school system to traditional family values of his people.

6. The Department of Indian Affairs apparently did nothing about the lack of educational opportunity, the lack of programs for mental health and alcohol treatment, and the abuses of power by his tribal government.

I then made a number of recommendations to prevent similar deaths, in which I pleaded for a commitment to end the tyranny that dominates and destroys the lives of young Aboriginals, for it is my view that the abysmal social conditions on Indian reserves in general continue unabated because there is nothing to control corrupt chiefs and councillors.

1. Prosecute crimes against Aboriginal people

I recommended that the provincial Department of Justice establish a Special Prosecutions Branch for the prosecution of crimes against Aboriginal people, and that this branch employ investigators from each of the Aboriginal language groups in Alberta so that investigations can be done in the language spoken by victims and accused persons. The branch should be given a mandate to prosecute all matters, from domestic assaults to racketeering, and this mandate should specifically include investigating and prosecuting any allegations within Indian & Northern Affairs Canada and tribal governments. The branch should be given unrestricted authority to decide what cases would be dealt with by way of alternative measures and restorative justice procedures, and which would be prosecuted in the usual manner.

I made this recommendation because in my view there is no legal mechanism for the prosecution of tribal government members who steal from their people, and my experience at Morley has satisfied me that thefts from public funds by chiefs are commonplace. In my view this was a very relevant factor in the death of Sherman Labelle because he was a "high needs" child and the necessary funding to provide for his needs was unavailable due to the misappropriation of funds by the tribal government of the day. The evidence at this fatality inquiry indicated a lack of programs, or weak programs, in mental health and alcohol counselling, no trauma counselling, a lack of facilities at the school, and even that the school gymnasium had been condemned for lack of maintenance. All of these problems relate to funding.

I referred to the investigation I had ordered in June of 1997, and my concerns about $50-million worth of timber that had been taken off the reserve without any of that money being paid to the tribal government and thus none of it being available for badly needed programs. This was a crime against the Stoney people, including Sherman Labelle, and nothing was done about it. I suggested that a Special Prosecutions Branch could begin with this matter.

I lamented the fact that in response to my order for an investigation, the Alberta Minister of Justice and Attorney General said that the problems were the jurisdiction not of Alberta but of Indian Affairs. I pointed out that he was incorrect to the extent that criminal activity anywhere in the province is the jurisdiction of the provincial Minister of Justice.

I referred to the 1996 report of the federal Auditor General, which had said there was $100-million unaccounted for in the Department of Indian Affairs. I warned that this created a very high risk of theft and fraud.

I quoted from the Cawsey Report, which had recommended the establishment of an Aboriginal Justice Commission that would have as part of its mandate:

(iii) To negotiate a framework agreement between the Government of Canada, the Government of Alberta, the Indians and the Métis which delineates the jurisdictional and financial responsibilities of the Government of Canada and the Government of Alberta toward Indians and Métis with respect to all components of the criminal justice system.

(iv) The Aboriginal Justice Commission would employ an Aboriginal advocate who would accept all complaints against any person or component of the criminal justice system, and who would ensure that all complaints are processed by existing complaint mechanisms in the criminal justice system.

In my study of the problems of Aboriginal peoples over the last few years, I am satisfied that there is a lack of recourse for them for wrongs committed against them. A large part of this problem is the confusion in federal and provincial jurisdiction. The Aboriginal Justice Commission recommended by Mr. Justice Cawsey, which was never implemented, would have gone a long way toward alleviating the problem. In my view, it is necessary to go further in order to give Aboriginal peoples the "equal protection of the law" to which they are entitled by section 15 of the Canadian Charter of Rights and Freedoms.

2. Legislate honesty in the public sector

Another recommendation was that the provincial government enact a statute that makes it an offence for any person who holds an elected position, or who is employed in the public sector, to make a false public statement.

I referred to my 1997 investigation order and said that the public statements made in response by politicians, INAC officials and others denying there was a problem, when there clearly was one, was a large part of the difficulty faced by Aboriginal people in their quest for justice.

3. Saturate Indian communities with wellness programs

I further recommended that the provincial Department of Health & Welfare unilaterally provide healthcare workers to reserve communities, and that all non-Aboriginal workers be required to have an Aboriginal person in training for their position, with a deadline for that Aboriginal person to take over the position.

Again I quoted the RCAP report, which had made a similar recommendation:

[that] federal, provincial and territorial governments col-

laborate with Aboriginal nations or communities, as appropriate, to

(a) develop a system of healing centres to provide services,
referral and access to specialist services;

(b) develop a network of healing lodges to provide residential
services oriented to the family and community healing;...

(d) mandate healing centres and lodges to provide
integrated health and social services in culturally
appropriate forms; and

(e) make the service network available to First Nations,
Inuit and Métis communities, in rural and urban
settings, on an equitable basis. (vol. 3, p. 241)

The problems of physical and mental health in reserve communities are approaching what will be a national disaster. The
issue whether this is the responsibility of the federal or provincial governments should not slow immediate steps to reverse the
downward spiral that is occurring.

4. Support Aboriginal education systems

My fourth recommendation was that the provincial government
unilaterally provide teachers and support staff to reserve schools
to ensure that the standards of education in those schools are
equivalent to provincial standards.

I made this recommendation because I was satisfied from the
evidence and from my observations on the reserve that abuses in
the education system were a major cause of the frustration and
despair that push so many young people to suicide. The chief of
the day was accused of using the education system as a "political
slush fund" and my belief is that this was a well-founded allegation.

5. Put an end to the ignorance about Aboriginal people

I further recommended that the provincial Department of Learning create courses in Aboriginal studies that will honestly and accurately tell the story of the history of Aboriginal peoples, their contributions, their world view, their cultures and the injustices they have suffered, and make these courses a mandatory part of the curriculum at all levels of grade school. Again I quoted from the Royal Commission on Aboriginal Peoples:

> We emphasize the need to correct erroneous assumptions and to dispel stereotypes that still abound in the minds of many Canadians, distorting their relationships with Aboriginal people. Accurate information about the history and cultures of Aboriginal peoples and nations, the role of treaties in the formation of Canada, and the distinctive contributions of Aboriginal people to contemporary Canada should form part of every Canadian student's education. (RCAP report, vol. 3, p. 489)

I set out my own experience in this regard: that I had been a judge for almost 20 years by the time of these events, yet knew virtually nothing about these people over whom I was exercising the power of a judge. I spoke of my commitment to educate myself about the Stoney people in particular and Aboriginal justice issues in general. What I learned was a most troubling lesson, but I firmly believe that if these matters are not generally known, the problems will continue; and I do not believe that the people of Canada would allow the plight of the Aboriginal people to continue if only they knew more about it.

6. Support the creation of broad-based First Nations governments

Another recommendation I made was that the provincial government provide funding for members of First Nations in Alberta to hold meetings for the purpose of uniting their local communities to form broad-based First Nations governments, and that the province consider creating electoral districts which would be comprised of groupings of Aboriginal communities so that there would be MLAs elected by an Aboriginal electorate.

Because I was conducting a fatality hearing under provincial legislation, the recommendations I would make would be to the provincial government, and this was now going far beyond that mandate, but it is a suggestion I think is worth pursuing.

Aboriginal people have very little representation in provincial legislatures and Parliament. With the notable exception of Manitoba's Elijah Harper – the first treaty Indian to be elected MLA and whose historic lone dissent in the Manitoba legislature defeated the Meech Lake constitutional accord in 1990 – Native people have very little opportunity to be heard. In this day and age of computer technology and multimedia information, it is really not necessary for political constituencies to be contiguous pieces of territory. My idea is that there could be a number of seats proportionate to Aboriginal populations that would be elected by Aboriginal people. Aboriginal voters would have the option to register to vote either in the Aboriginal constituency or in the general constituency, as is done, for example, by the Māori in New Zealand.

As it is now, the Canadian Aboriginal vote is fragmented to such an extent that it has little or no effect on the outcome of elections. If the Aboriginal communities were grouped so that the grouping could elect an MLA or MP, it would give them a voice they currently do not have.

With regard to the Stoney in particular, I believe the biggest obstacle impeding social and economic development at Morley is the division of the community into the three separate bands. I believe this applies to reserve communities everywhere. The isolation of these communities from one another precludes them from obtaining the advantages they could realize from pooling their resources. If all of the reserves in a given area were to elect one MLA it would create the opportunity to deal with issues co-operatively as well as giving the people a voice.

The RCAP report had this to say about the distinction between the term First Nation and local community:

> First Nations hold differing views regarding the most appropriate level for governmental institutions. These differences are reflected in the varying ways in which the term First Nation is used. Sometimes it is used in a broad sense to indicate a body of Indian people whose members have a shared sense of national identity based on a common heritage, situation and outlook, including such elements as history, language, culture, spirituality, ancestry and homeland. Under this usage, a First Nation would often be composed of a number of local communities living on distinct territorial bases. However, in other instances the term First Nation is used in a narrow sense to identify a single local community of Indian people living on its own territorial base, often a reserve governed by the Indian Act. (vol. 2, p. 157)

> The Commission concludes that the right of self-determination is vested in Aboriginal nations rather than small local communities. By Aboriginal nation we mean a sizable body of Aboriginal people with a shared sense of national identity that constitutes the predominant population in a certain territory or group of territories. Currently there are between 60 and 80 historically based nations in Canada, compared with a thousand or so local Aboriginal communities. (vol. 2, p. 166)

> The Commission therefore recommends that ... All governments in Canada recognize that the right of self-governance

is vested in Aboriginal nations rather than small local communities. (vol. 2, p. 236)

I believe that the formation of First Nations governments in the larger sense described by the Royal Commission would make it more difficult to perpetrate the abuses of power that occur in small communities where one family is often able to dominate. Also, larger nations would have the capacity to create institutions which would be a recourse for members of the local communities.

I believe that if groups of reserve communities were to make up a single electoral district, established political parties would become more active in those Aboriginal communities, and that this would both educate the people in relation to real democracy and give them a voice in government.

7. Support the abolition of INAC

My seventh recommendation was that the provincial government support the abolition of Indian & Northern Affairs Canada. I set out my belief that the corruption which seems so prevalent on Indian reserves could not happen without the knowledge and even the complicity of the officials in the Department of Indian Affairs.

Witnesses at the inquiry spoke of the department being unwilling or unable to help with the problems on the reserve, and that money that comes through the department never reaches the people for whom it is intended.

8. Support economic development in Aboriginal communities

Indian reserves are a fact of life. Our predecessors established them as holding places for the Indians, to be used only as long as necessary to assimilate the Indians into the general population. Many reserves have become violent, dysfunctional ghettos with rates of crime and suicide ten times those of the general population. So what should be done about it? One suggestion is just to divide up the land, give individual titles and let the owners sell it off. I believe this would be a disaster, that it would only take a few years for the dishonest and unscrupulous to take away the property of the naïve and the dysfunctional, and that it would be a complete failure by the government of Canada to discharge its obligations to the Aboriginal people of Canada.

I believe the only solution is to make these dysfunctional communities into healthy places and that the only way this can happen is to make them economically viable. This is not being accomplished by dishing out millions of dollars to tribal governments so that they can spend it on trips to Las Vegas. The Royal Commission report confirms this thinking:

> Three problems need to be solved to create a safe environment for development. First, a way needs to be found to separate and limit powers. If power is concentrated in a few hands, and if there are few constraints on its exercise, there is a strong risk that those with power will use it in their own interests, possibly at the expense of others in the community. Second, there must be a means to settle disputes that is open and impartial and provides the assurance of a fair hearing, with judgment rendered by a body not controlled by government or any community faction. Third, a way needs to be found to guard against inappropriate political involvement in the day-to-day decisions of business ventures or economic development institutions. (vol. 2, p. 481)

9. Demand accountability in Aboriginal matters

My final recommendation was that the provincial government should demand that the federal government and INAC put strict guidelines on the money they pay out so that it goes to people for whom it is intended. I found support for this in the following statement in the RCAP report:

> Governments with the authority and responsibility to spend public funds for particular purposes should be held accountable for such expenditures, primarily by their citizens and also by other governments from which they receive fiscal transfers. In the context of Aboriginal governments, it is our view that this accountability rests with the Aboriginal nation rather than with individual communities. Funding arrangements should reflect this basic objective, allowing for processes and systems of accountability that are both explicit and transparent. (vol. 2, p. 282)

At present it is extremely difficult to prosecute fraudulent transactions in Aboriginal matters, because there are insufficient controls and guidelines on how money is to be used. While there are not yet First Nations governments to demand this accountability from local communities, it is all the more necessary that the federal government provide guidelines and controls.

I concluded my fatality inquiry report with the following summary:

> Suicides among Aboriginal young people are the result of the history of injustices they have suffered and continue to suffer. In order to prevent similar deaths, the injustices must be eliminated. I have herein set out the first steps that I believe should be taken in this regard.

Finally, I acknowledged the federal government for establishing the Royal Commission on Aboriginal Peoples. The report of this commission is an exhaustive work on the history and condition of the Aboriginal people of Canada and was of great assistance to me in my efforts to understand the Aboriginal people and Aboriginal justice issues. My only difficulty with the RCAP report is that the material becomes buried in its own length, and that is why I have here extracted portions that I believed to be most relevant to the condition of Aboriginal people in relation to the death of Sherman Labelle.

I signed and dated the Labelle fatality inquiry report on September 16, 1999. From the vantage point of today, 11 years later, I would only add that I doubt anyone in the provincial Department of Justice or the federal Department of Indian & Northern Affairs ever read the Sherman Labelle fatality report. The fact that the Stoney tribal administration filed a complaint about me because of some of the things I said in it at least gave me the satisfaction of knowing that someone at Morley had read it.

On further reflection I would add the recommendation that programs be established or research done to assist Aboriginal people in adaptation to white society, as opposed to assimilation into white society. It is unrealistic to think that the way of life the Aboriginal people had at the time of the treaties could have been preserved, and it certainly cannot be recreated in today's world, because the whole world has changed. I believe that many young Aboriginals are confused by the message that life should be as it was, and therefore they do not adapt to life as it is. Serious work must be done to help them adapt to life as it is today.

❖ 16 ❖

BAD MEDICINE

What were the results of my efforts? Some significant health concerns. These may have been the stress getting to me or they may have been due to experiencing some bad medicine. On October 6, 1998, while presiding at the court in Cochrane, I began to feel ill. My chest hurt, I was short of breath and I felt faint. I told the clerk I wanted to adjourn for a few minutes, got up and went to my office. I must have looked awful because the clerk became very anxious and insisted on calling an ambulance.

The judge's office in Cochrane is across a back hall from the courtroom, but the courtroom door and the office door line up so that if they are both open there is a clear line of vision from the courtroom into the office. Inside the office door was a couch where I lay down. Both doors were left open. Marjorie Powderface came into the office and stood at the end of the couch so that she was between me and the courtroom. Marjorie told me the next day that she had placed herself between me and René Calfchild because she believed he was using medicine against me.

Before court that morning, I had gone into the Coffee Trader for my usual cup of tea. Calfchild had followed me in and walked around me. He said to me, "I don't want to ever appear in front of you again." Later he sat in the front row of the courtroom and stared at me throughout the proceedings until I adjourned. Calfchild had been in court on charges that he had raped Marjorie's mother. The matter never went to trial because the victim was not able to testify.

The medics arrived and tended to me. My heart rate and blood pressure were both unusually high. They used a field EKG, which did not indicate a problem. However, they said I should go to hospital, as they were concerned about my heart rate and blood pressure and said the field equipment was not completely reliable.

I agreed to have them take me to the hospital in Canmore, and they did so. En route I could feel my symptoms easing and by the time I got there I felt reasonably well. Blood samples were taken and I was monitored for a few hours and released with instructions to see my family doctor.

While I was with the medics and at the hospital, Rose Auger had gone to my home. Marjorie had told her about the incident in Cochrane, which she was sure was the result of bad medicine. Rose had left instructions that I was to come and see her the next day.

I went out to see Rose the next morning and her sons, Dale and George (Cha Chee), were there preparing the rocks for a sweat. Marjorie came and we prayed together in the sweat lodge with Rose and Dale.

Dale and Cha Chee were probably Rose's greatest success and greatest failure respectively. Dale had earned a PhD in education and was an amazing visual artist as well as being a traditional pipe carrier – a person qualified in his tradition to preside at pipe ceremonies. Cha Chee was an alcoholic with an extensive criminal record. When Rose died on July 30, 2006, Dale presided over a traditional Cree burial, which began in the evening and went all night with interment the next morning. Cha Chee was brought from prison to attend.

On October 7 I went to see my family doctor, who recommended that I take a leave of absence, which I did. Except for appearances to complete matters that I had outstanding I did not return to work until February of 1999. One of the first matters I presided over when I returned was the Sherman Labelle fatality inquiry.

I received many invitations to speak on the subject of Aboriginal justice and accountability. On April 15, 1998, at the invitation of Professor Tony Hall, I spoke at the University of Lethbridge on "The Law of the Crown in Indian Country." One of the people in attendance was Harley Frank, who had been chief of the Kainai First Nation. I answered a number of questions during the forum, and at first Harley seemed offended by the fact that I was speaking in relation to my knowledge of Aboriginal traditions and justice. But by the end of the forum he said something that I took as a great compliment. He said I reminded him of the character in the film *Dances with Wolves*: when the cavalry came and found the character played by Kevin Costner, they said, "He's gone Injun on us."

I was again asked to speak at a forum at the University of Lethbridge on January 19, 2000. The forum was entitled "The Changing Face of Aboriginal Politics in the 21st Century." I shared the dais with Myron Thompson, who at the time was the MP for the constituency of Wildrose, which includes the reserve at Morley.

After the forum, Harley came and asked me if I would agree to a prayer ceremony with the Kainai elders John Chief Moon and Floyd Manyfingers. I agreed and we went to my room in the Lethbridge Lodge hotel.

In the ceremony, John Chief Moon told me he would offer me an eagle feather three times. I would reach for it each time, but he would not give it to me until the third time. I remember trying to focus on the ceremony, but I was very concerned about burning sweet grass, which I was afraid might set off the smoke alarm in my non-smoking room, and beating on a drum, which I was afraid might be disturbing my neighbours. It made it difficult to concentrate on the ceremony, but I did the best I could. At the end of the ceremony, the eagle feather was given to me. We then had tea and John Chief Moon told me that I could use the feather to brush away any bad medicine but that I must never use it to try to send the bad medicine back to whoever is sending it. This he said could be very dangerous for me.

When I returned to Morley, the elder Bill McLean was very concerned about me. He told me he had been invited to a prayer ceremony at the home of John Stevens, the medicine man. He told me that John Snow and Lazarus Wesley were there, and that he learned that the purpose of the ceremony was to invoke a bad medicine against me, Greg Twoyoungmen and others. Bill told me it was necessary for me to get protection from this bad medicine. Greg also contacted me to tell me he had heard about the ceremony and that I needed protection.

I don't entirely disbelieve the possibility that there are people who can invoke bad medicine in a way that will do harm, and I certainly didn't want to ignore what Bill and Greg were saying. I told them I was confident I was protected because John Chief Moon had done an eagle feather ceremony for me and I had the eagle feather he had presented to me in that ceremony. This seemed to satisfy them, and I will admit that it also reassured me that if there was a real danger presented by the medicine, I would be protected from it.

I absolutely believe in the power of prayer. I believe John Chief Moon is a good and holy man, and I believe his prayers helped to sustain me through some very difficult years.

I was told later that the ceremony at Stevens's home had backfired on its participants. John Snow's niece had died. Lazarus had suffered a stroke. Stevens himself had fallen into a dry well and been trapped there all day. I don't confirm or dispute these things. This is what I was told. I do know that many people on the reserve believe it.

❖ 17 ❖

THE CHIEFS COMPLAIN

By a letter dated October 6, 1999, on Stoney tribal administration stationery, the three chiefs – D'Arcy Dixon of the Bearspaw, Paul Chiniquay of the Chiniki and John Snow of the Wesley – made a formal complaint about my findings in the Sherman Labelle inquiry.

My reading of the letter was that they simply didn't think I had enough evidence to prove the statements I had made in the report. They complained they were not given an opportunity to respond or give evidence. I found it amusing that Chief D'Arcy Dixon signed the letter when he himself had testified. He was the chief I referred to in my report, a member of the education committee sending his own children to off-reserve schools.

In my view, the really unfortunate aspect of the chiefs' letter was that they did not deny any of my statements or speak of anything that would prove me wrong. It appeared to me to be a confirmation of what I had said. The Judicial Council dismissed this complaint, but it was only one arrow in John Snow's quiver.

Ernest Hunter had been released from prison in September of that year. Prior to being sent to jail by the Court of Appeal he had been bragging to people on the reserve that he had made a deal with me that had kept him out of jail. He evidently told people that I had promised him no jail in return for information about John Snow. Snow apparently heard about this and spoke to Hunter about it. On September 10, 1999, Snow had Hunter taken to the law offices of Terry Munro & Associates, where Hunter swore a statutory declaration setting out the allegations. This statutory declaration was sent to the chief judge of the Alberta Provincial Court by a letter dated October 21.

When I received copies from the chief judge, I thought it was curious that the letter had been sent more than a month after the declaration had been sworn. I also thought the timing with the letter from the three chiefs was curious. It became apparent that John Snow had orchestrated both.

Hunter had been given the statutory declaration after swearing it and was to send it to the chief judge. He of course knew the allegations were false and he burned the document. Only after the letter from the three chiefs was sent was it discovered that Hunter's statutory declaration had not been received by the chief judge's office. Evidently there had been some exchange of information between the chiefs and the chief judge that made the chiefs realize Hunter had not forwarded the statutory declaration. So, John Snow sent Terry Munro out to find Hunter. Munro prepared the cover letter, had Hunter sign it, and forwarded it himself.

The chief judge convened and chaired a meeting of the Judicial Council to determine what was to be done with the statutory declaration. The Judicial Council had three alternatives: take no action; reprimand me; or refer the matter to a judicial inquiry board. The most onerous measure was the third, since it is a condition precedent to the removal of a judge from office, and that is the alternative the council chose. In my view, that hearing was a judicial process. I was entitled to notice of the hearing, the right to be heard and the right to be represented by counsel. I was given none of those things. I was simply advised of the *fait accompli*.

My lawyer, Alan Hunter, QC, and I discussed applying for a judicial review of the decision of the Judicial Council. We decided not to, because it seemed easier to just appear before the inquiry board and trust that the absurd allegations being made would not prevail. However, we prepared for the hearing as if every allegation would be taken seriously and would have to be met.

When the day arrived for the hearing, Ernest Hunter was to be the first witness. He did not attend. The hearing was adjourned to the next day and the board issued a warrant for his arrest. On the following day he was brought into the hearing in prison garb and questioned on his statutory declaration. He repudiated all of the allegations.

I believe the horrible waste of time, and of tens of thousands of dollars in taxpayers' money, could have been avoided if the chief judge had simply interviewed Hunter, or had him interviewed, and discovered the complete lack of merit to the complaint. I believe that the peremptory proceeding he took was motivated by our ongoing conflict, an ongoing desire to "shut me up," and that it demonstrated his complete lack of concern for procedural fairness.

When the judicial inquiry board released its findings, which completely exonerated me, I wrote a letter to the Judicial Council suggesting to them that since the content of the statutory declaration had been repudiated, and since the council had acted on the perjured statutory declaration, they should refer the matter to the RCMP for investigation. This was done, and in due course the RCMP contacted me. I told them of the involvement by Snow and Terry Munro and suggested that they were the prime movers in the preparation and delivery of the perjured declaration, and that they should be the ones to be charged.

The RCMP conducted an investigation that consisted of interviewing Snow, Munro and Hunter. Hunter would not state that Snow and Munro knew the allegations were false, and in any event it had been established that he was a completely unreliable witness no matter what he said. So the only one charged was Ernest Hunter.

Hunter pleaded guilty to a charge of attempted obstruction of justice, and I was asked for a victim impact statement. I was, after all, the victim of his crime. It was my view by this time that Hunter had been used and abused sufficiently. I had caused him great difficulty by using his case to attempt to establish a precedent in relation to the "circumstances of Aboriginal offenders." I wrote a victim impact statement which was an attempt to mitigate any sentence he might receive. The prosecutor in the case wrote to me subsequently to tell me that this case was dealt with along with other charges against him, and Hunter basically received no additional penalty because of the false statutory declaration.

Snow attempted to vindicate himself from the allegations I had made against him, by bringing a motion before the Stoney tribal council. On May 14, 2000, he asked the council to demand a formal apology from me for remarks I had made. His motion was defeated 13 to 2. My old friend Tina Fox told me she had been the first to speak to the motion, and that she had said she would not ask anyone to apologize for speaking the truth. Greg Twoyoungmen also spoke to the motion and said it was John Snow who should apologize to me and his people for the millions of dollars of his people's money that he spent frivolously.

The final complaint came from the Reverend Dr. Chief John Snow himself, on October 25, 2000. He basically reiterated his former complaints about the Hunter case and the Labelle inquiry. The Judicial Council advised him that the matters had been dealt with, and dismissed his complaint.

❖ 18 ❖

THE AFTERMATH

In August of 2003 I was again invited back to Lethbridge, to be officially inducted into the Kainai Nation. John Chief Moon and Floyd Manyfingers conducted a ceremony on the bluff overlooking the Lethbridge coulee. They gave me the name Ninnaipoyii, which means Chief Speaker. John Chief Moon said his people have complained for years about the injustices I spoke of, but no one hears them. He told me they gave me this name because I spoke for them and for their children. It was a deeply humbling experience.

I got some good press. In addition to all the media coverage referred to in chapter 12, I was the subject of a feature article by Gordon Laird in *Saturday Night* magazine, a cover story in *Canadian Lawyer* and a full-page article in *The Washington Post*.

Cochrane This Week, now the *Cochrane Times*, gave me an award for Newsmaker of the Year for 1998. The Cochrane Rotary Club gave me their Integrity Award at a dinner at the Western Heritage Centre on February 26, 1999, and the Centennial Rotary Club in Calgary gave me their Integrity Award for 2002.

Tina Fox retired from the tribal council at the end of 2000 and went to Brandon, Manitoba, to pursue a degree in First Nations and Aboriginal counselling. She graduated in May 2003 and has been working as a counsellor at the Morley community school since.

Marlon House had his picture in the *Cochrane Eagle* a few weeks ago. He was playing in a music festival. Life seems to go on as if nothing had happened.

I see Ernest Hunter at round dances from time to time. Every time I see him, he is in the company of two women. He evidently has some charm. Even Rondi Lefthand said he was a good man when he wasn't drinking. He has had a number of further charges and I wonder what his situation would have been if the Court of Appeal had just left him on probation rather than sending him back to jail. I don't think he understands very much about the legal proceedings he has been involved in.

Baret Labelle has been back in court a few times. He seemed to appreciate the tremendous break he received in relation to the aggravated assault on John Anderson, but he continues to live in the toxic environment at Morley and he still struggles with his demons.

Unfortunately, Ernest Wesley and I had a falling-out. I was hopeful that when he was re-elected he would re-establish the Nakoda Education Management Team and the SITE program. It seemed he was more bitter toward the other chiefs than he was toward John Snow. He had decided that the only way to govern was to completely separate the Wesley, Bearspaw and Chiniki. In my view, the separation that already existed was one of the most harmful aspects of life on the Stoney reserve.

There had been an attempt once before to have just one chief, in the 1970s. John Snow had run against Frank Kaquitts, a Chiniki. Frank won the election and became chief of all of the Stoneys for a time. John Snow realized he could not win an election on the reserve as a whole, so he told people that three chiefs had signed the treaty and that if the Stoneys did not have three chiefs they would lose their treaty rights. In my view this was the most selfish, harmful lie that has ever been told in this community.

The three-way division of the community multiplies administration costs and makes it almost impossible for any one of the three divisions to create a successful program to deal with the alcohol addiction, the family violence or any of the other badly needed initiatives that might generate an improvement in wellness.

Wesley even wanted to divide the school into three. When this proposal was discussed, Tina Fox told me she spoke to the proposal and said, "I have grandchildren in the Wesley, the Bearspaw and the Chiniki. How do I divide up my grandchildren?" Tina's sentiments carried the day, and the school, at least, remains one. Ernest lost the next election and I haven't seen him since.

One good thing Ernest did was hire Yvonne DePeel as the superintendent for the Stoney Education Authority. Yvonne has worked tirelessly to improve education at the schools on the Stoney reserves at Morley and also at Big Horn, near Nordegg, Alberta, and at Eden Valley, a reserve near Longview. Her efforts have paid off and there are bigger classes every year graduating from Grade 12 and more and more Stoneys going on to higher education.

I officially retired as a Provincial Court judge in 2008, even though I continue to sit as a supernumerary judge. I had a retirement dinner at the Glen Eagles golf course in October of that year. The dinner was attended by about 200 people, mostly lawyers but also a number of elders from Morley. I asked that, instead of gifts, the attendees make donations to the Stoney Education Project.

I had asked Yvonne what she would like to be able to buy for the school if I could raise a sum of money for her. She said the school had a computer-assisted learning program, called Fast

Forward, for the higher grades but not for kindergarten to Grade 3. She said the program could advance a student a full grade level in eight weeks. It would cost about $20,000. My dinner raised about $5,000, which was donated in my name, and I matched it. The $10,000 was again matched by Bill Hartman of Shaman Resources and so I was able to make that small contribution to Stoney Education.

In the fall that year, the University of Calgary had an educational conference at Lake Louise. The conference dealt with the different ways in which different cultures learn, and was attended by world-renowned educators. Yvonne managed to get a number of the speakers to come to a seminar at which many of the teachers from Treaty 7 schools were in attendance. It was a great opportunity. I was able to present Yvonne with a cheque for the Fast Forward computer program and speak to the gathering of about 200 educators. I told them: "Statistics show that Aboriginal young people are more likely to go to jail than to finish Grade 12. So your work is not just advancing their education, it is keeping them out of jail." Yvonne told me that this became the theme of the conference.

❖ 19 ❖

REFLECTIONS

Fourteen years have passed since I began my crusade to improve the delivery of justice to the Stoney. Was it worth it for me? Absolutely. My life became much harder but much better.

Being a judge is about as hard as you make it. My old friend Norm Mackie, who was appointed a few years before I was, said he liked being a judge because "it was like watching television, only you got to write in your own endings."

Some judges are jerks. They use their authority to bully lawyers and witnesses and anyone else who comes into their court. They impose draconian sentences, thinking they are going to stamp out crime, and all they really do is make people avoid them.

Before I was appointed, I had worked with Michael Starr, a prominent defence lawyer. He said he had a couple of elective surgeries he was putting off for the day when he really needed an adjournment because Judge X was presiding. He said that if he had a client who was willing to pay, he'd have his tonsils or his appendix out, in order for his client to avoid a particular judge. Those judges show up in court and their lists disappear. They are done for the morning 15 minutes after court is scheduled to start, because everything is adjourned. Other judges make a real effort to do what is right.

Judges have a tremendous power. They have the power to take away a person's freedom, the most important thing that we have in a free and democratic society.

Before my education in Stoney, I was a lazy judge who just

applied the law as if it were a mathematical formula. I read the headnotes of the Court of Appeal decisions and I knew what they wanted and I gave it to them. For the first 15 years that I sat as a judge, I did my work as if I were a law student back at university. To get through university, you figure out what the professor wants and you give it to him, whether you agree with it or not. To be a successful lower-court judge, you figure out what the Court of Appeal wants and you give it to them, whether you agree with it or not.

That day in the spring of 1997, in the Wesley cemetery, with the crocuses blooming and the spirits of all those young Stoneys hovering around me, my life changed forever. I could no longer be that complacent jerk applying the law without regard to the effect I was having on these people.

Rupert Ross spoke of an Oji-Cree elder who said that it isn't the abuse of power that is a problem, it is the very fact that people have power over others that is wrong. Perhaps I should have just resigned my position as a judge. Then I would no longer have the power that I now see as wrong. But resigning wouldn't change the system. So I have stayed and tried to exercise the power of my office with compassion and understanding. I write a judgment every once in a while just to explain the futility of imprisonment to the Court of Appeal. If they read them at all, they don't seem to pay any attention.

I think that my name, John, is appropriate. I often feel like John the Baptist – a voice crying in the wilderness. A lot of people have since heard the message of the Baptist. Perhaps one day my message will be accepted, and the legal system, and society in general, will see the advantage of dealing with the underlying causes of crime rather than punishing the results of those underlying causes. If that ever happens, we may truly create that just peaceful and safe society which our Criminal Code says is the fundamental purpose of sentencing. When my time comes, the Creator may overlook my other shortcomings and welcome me into the spirit world because I cared about my Stoney relations.

And what do I think about John Snow? He too was the victim of his circumstances, and as I have said, "circumstances" has become the byword of my life. Snow grew up in Canada. But he did not grow up in a free and democratic society like most Canadians do. He grew up in an absolute dictatorship created by the government of Canada. He grew up on an Indian reserve that was ruled by an Indian agent who had the power to control every aspect of his life. The Indian agent received all of the money and rations that were allotted to the "Indian tribe," and he had absolute say in who got what. He could control the whole tribe by cultivating the support of one or two families, who would then help control the others. He would do this by giving them more rations and more privileges than the others, and this became "tribal custom."

Snow went to a school where none of his teachers spoke his language and where he was punished if he spoke it himself. The school was designed to take the Indian out of the Indian child. It taught that Indians were substandard human beings and that the only way to escape being substandard was to become a white man. So Snow became a white man. He got a white man's education and he became a minister of the United Church, the kind of white man that had the power and authority in his world. When Snow became chief – the first chief after the removal of the Indian agent – the only role model he had for governance was the Indian agent, and he became that too. He developed a sense of entitlement and the same contempt for the Indians that he saw in the white men that had gone before. Warren Harbeck told me that in conversations he had overheard between Snow and his wife, his wife would refer to the "stupid Stoneys."

As chief, Snow received all of the money that came from Ottawa. He had control of it and he could use it as he saw fit. First of all, he would look after himself and his family, and then, when he had sated himself and his family, he would dole out what was left to the others. He didn't see anything wrong with this because it was what he had grown up with and what he had learned. We learn what we live. We live what we learn.

What about Marlon House? How could his parents have allowed their 30-year-old son to bring home a 14-year-old girl and abuse her in their presence? In my judicial sittings, I had occasion to have his father appear in court charged with the sexual exploitation of a young girl who was on his school bus. The father too was a school bus driver. One can only imagine what abuses Marlon grew up with. We live what we learn. We learn what we live.

My biggest disappointment is that the Court of Appeal has never really dealt with my basic proposition, which is that these people come from such dysfunction that it is an injustice to punish them for being dysfunctional. The learned higher court justices study the law and know the precedents, but the problem with a system based on precedents is that if you were wrong before, you keep making the same mistakes. My view is that the reliance on denunciation and deterrence that is so firmly supported by the precedents is archaic and wrong. If our objective in criminal law is simply to punish crime, then we should just say so and that would be the end of it. But this is not what the Criminal Code says. The Criminal Code says:

> 718. The fundamental purpose of sentencing is to contribute, along with crime prevention initiatives, to respect for the law and the maintenance of a just, peaceful and safe society by imposing just sanctions that have one or more of the following objectives:...

718.2 ...

(e) all available sanctions other than imprisonment that are
reasonable in the circumstances should be considered
for all offenders, with particular attention to the
circumstances of aboriginal offenders.

Unfortunately, the objectives also include "to denounce" and "to
deter," and that brings up precedents that go back to the Middle
Ages, when the only method of behaviour modification known to
man was to attempt to instill fear by the use of draconian penalties.

I say that we have a choice as to what we want to do in relation
to offenders. We must choose whether we want to punish crime
or reduce crime. If we just want to punish crime, then we can use
denunciation and deterrence to our hearts' content. If we want
to reduce crime, which in my view is the better way to *contribute
to the maintenance of a just, peaceful and safe society*, the process
becomes much more complicated and much more difficult.

Does punishing crime really reduce crime? Does deterrence
really work? There is an abundance of writing by psychologists
and criminologists that support the view that prison sentences
have a very limited deterrent effect. My own opinion, after more
than 30 years of presiding in criminal courts, is that sending people to prison on the pretence of deterring crime is futile, wasteful
and counterproductive.

Prisons have their place. There are people who are a danger to
other members of society and they should be locked up for the
protection of the public. There are people who are incorrigible
repeat offenders and they should be locked up from time to time
to give the public a respite from their activities.

I believe Marlon House to be a cruel sociopath who had a
need to control women and who controlled them with brutality. I
sentenced him to the longest period of imprisonment I thought

I could justify, in order to protect Cynthia Beaver and any other woman that might come under his power. The Court of Appeal said it was too much.

I sentenced Baret Labelle to probation because I saw him as a disadvantaged young man, the child of an alcoholic mother, suffering from a speech impediment, easily led astray by an older peer. In my view he was someone who needed help, not punishment. I employed a sanction that I thought would help him. The Court of Appeal said I was wrong for not sending him to jail. Fortunately, by the time his case was heard in the Court of Appeal, he had successfully completed the probation and was said to be doing well. The court only grudgingly agreed not to resentence him, because of subsequent circumstances.

I did my best to write a judgment that would put all of the information I had about him and his community "on the record" so that the Court of Appeal could see the huge disadvantages facing this boy. Why could they not see that what I had done was the right thing to do? I think they should have said: "This worked! It's evidently better than sending him to jail. We uphold this decision because it has contributed to the just, peaceful and safe society, and that is the fundamental purpose of sentencing."

Why didn't they say this? I say it is because the whole system has been so hung up on punishment for so long that to let go of it would be to admit we have been wrong for hundreds of years. It is easier to continue to make the error than to admit the error.

Sending this disadvantaged young man to prison would likely have brutalized him. It would at the very least have been a setback in his development. Prisons are fertile places for gangs. A person like Baret would likely have had to look to gang members for protection, and then he would be a member when he came out. The harm that prisons do is undeniable, and the likelihood was high that Baret Labelle would come out worse than he went in.

The fear, which in my view is paranoia, is that if you don't punish everyone who commits an offence, you will "open the floodgates." Suddenly there will be thousands of similar assaults because there will be no deterrence. In reality (the reality that only seems to exist outside of the law books), the reason why most people who don't commit assaults don't commit them is because they have no inclination to do so. Those that are inclined to do so commit them in spite of the law and the penalties.

What do I think of former Chief Judge Edward R. Wachowich? I last saw Ed just before Christmas 2009. Judge David Tilley and I had been friends since university, and Dave died on December 4. Laura and I went up to Edmonton for the celebration of Dave's life and Ed was there. We spoke briefly. He and Dave had played sports pools and Ed had become concerned because he had left a message on the Tilleys' answering machine about Dave losing a bet. He discovered later that Dave was already dead when he left the message. Poor Ed: even though he caused me a lot of aggravation, I was never able to generate serious anger toward him, because I felt sorry for him.

He was right about one thing, though. He accused me of losing my objectivity with Aboriginal offenders, and that was correct. I also lost my ignorance about them, which in my view is a necessary ingredient of the objectivity. I believe I replaced objectivity and ignorance with knowledge and compassion. If that's a bad thing, I'm going to stick with it anyway.

What do I think of former Chief Crown Prosecutor Bruce Fraser? He is now a Provincial Court judge and we greet each other in the courthouse from time to time. When I asked him to appoint a full-time prosecutor to Cochrane, I was thinking about improving the quality of justice for offenders and victims. I have never had an administrative position, so I have no appreciation of what difficulties he would have encountered administratively to take my suggestion. Prosecutors are in fact being assigned to the various circuit courts on a more permanent basis now. Sometimes it works better and sometimes not, depending on the personality of the person assigned.

What do I think of tribal governments? Some don't want change. As long as their people are uneducated and ignorant they are easy to control and exploit. It takes exceptional leaders to overcome the temptation to just look after themselves, and to work for the betterment of their whole community.

What do I think of the government of Canada? I believe that politicians are afraid to acknowledge the magnitude of the problem. The dysfunction in Canada's Aboriginal population – the violence, alcoholism, prescription drug abuse, political corruption, fetal-alcohol children, children in care, illiteracy, unemployment, suicides – the list goes on and on. The causes are as complex as the solutions, but the government doesn't work toward solutions because they are afraid to admit responsibility for the causes. So they say they are not going to interfere. They will treat Aboriginals as independent nations. This is the biggest cop-out of all, because Aboriginals have been so crippled by the history of abuse that they cannot overcome their past without outside help.

What do I think of the government of Alberta? In Canada's confederal system, the provinces are responsible for the investigation and prosecution of crime. The federal government is responsible for Indian affairs. If Indian chiefs are stealing from their people, it is a crime that should be investigated and prosecuted by the provincial government. But the provincial law enforcement agencies don't prosecute, because they take the position that it is a matter for Indian Affairs.

When the *Calgary Herald* reported that Chief Philomene Stevens had used her position with Child & Family Services to pay for a nanny for her children [see p. 188], it must have been a documented fact or they would not have printed it. The paper would not have exposed itself to the liability. If any public figure in any town or village in Canada had done what Chief Stevens did, there is no doubt they would have been prosecuted for the theft of public moneys, and the prosecution would have been seeking imprisonment because it was a trust theft. On an Indian reserve it is overlooked. The result is that children who require services, and don't get them because of a lack of funding, do not have the protection of the law. The only way this will change is for the provincial and federal governments to work together.

I remember my father quoting Jesus. When the woman brought perfume for Jesus's feet, Judas said the money would have been better used for the poor. Jesus replied, "The poor you will have always with you." My father's interpretation of this was that we will never eradicate poverty, but we must keep trying. The dysfunction in Aboriginal communities may be with us for a long time, but we must keep working toward overcoming it.

What do I think about Aboriginal offenders? My thinking has not just changed in relation to Aboriginal offenders, it has changed with regard to all offenders. After more than 30 years of presiding in criminal courts it is my observation that the vast majority of people who have come before me as accused persons are not bad people so much as they are disadvantaged people. I believe that the reason why Aboriginal people are so overrepresented in the prison system and the criminal justice system is that they are overrepresented among the poor and the disadvantaged. I believe the majority of the people who appear before me need help.

When I hear politicians and lawmakers talking about the need for greater penalties, I believe they are simply ignorant of the true situation or they are catering to a populace that seeks vengeance and retribution rather than solutions to social problems.

I believe that the populist view comes from a perception that all criminals are like Bonnie and Clyde or Paul Bernardo and Karla Homolka. I have seen very few people in all my years on the bench who are really bad. The vast majority are alcoholics whose lives are out of control. Periods of imprisonment, which unquestionably are a popular way of dealing with offending behaviour, may do more harm than good.

This is the different understanding I have come to as a result of my years of Stoney immersion. I think I am a better person for the education I have received from my Stoney relations. I think our society as a whole would be better if more people could learn what I have learned. I would like to live to see the "just, peaceful and safe society" of which our Criminal Code speaks. Perhaps I will see it from the spirit world. Perhaps one day the good medicine will overcome the bad.

EPILOGUE:
THE RETURN OF BAD MEDICINE

One of the differences between white men and red men is that white
men have organized crime and red men have chief and council.
— DON BURNSTICK

When I finished the manuscript for this book in February of 2010 I was feeling hopeful for the future of the Stoney people at Morley. That hope was based mostly on the tremendous improvement I had seen in education.

Barely a month later, however, my optimism was shattered when I was informed that Yvonne DePeel, the superintendent of schools for the Stoney Education Authority, had been fired. The three chiefs had hired a new CEO of the tribal administration, Greg Varricchio, who said he was taking education in a new direction and that he didn't really fire DePeel, just "unhired" her.

I was personally devastated. The huge and hopeful improvement I had seen in the schools at Morley had taken place over the nine years in which Yvonne DePeel was the superintendent.

I recall visiting the community school in the years before Yvonne. The building was poorly maintained, the students badly behaved, the morale of the staff low. It was said the school was being used as a political slush fund. Jobs were given to friends of the chief, who were not even expected to show up for work in order to collect their salaries. The suspicion was that large portions of those unearned salaries were given back to the chief, allowing him to show expenditures in education which were in fact going into his pocket. This system was a double win for the chief. He got the money and kept his people uneducated too. He sent his own children to off-reserve schools and then to university, the plan being to have his progeny continue to dominate the people for years to come.

When Ernest Wesley was elected in 1992 he made a concerted effort to improve the education of his people, through SITE – Self Improvement Through Education – and he generated a significant improvement in education during the four years that he was chief. The school was operated by a committee, and an adult education program was created that had over 100 adults enrolled.

Then, in 1996, the Reverend Dr. Chief John Snow was re-elected. He terminated the employment of almost 100 people, including teachers and other school staff. Chaos returned to the school and the adult education program was discontinued.

In 2000, when Ernest Wesley again defeated John Snow, I expected he would reinstate his SITE program and pick up where he had left off. Unfortunately, Ernest was embittered by the destruction of his programs and blamed the Chiniki and Bearspaw chiefs for not standing up to Snow. He became obsessed with separating the three bands, each of which was now calling itself a First Nation. He even advocated that anyone who was not a member of the Wesley First Nation should be moved to the south side of the Bow River, so that only Wesleys would occupy the area north of the river.

Ernest called himself chief of the Wesley First Nation. I addressed correspondence to him as chief of the Wesley division of the Stoney Nakoda First Nation. Unfortunately, he didn't see any humour in my title for him and this became an unresolvable obstacle in our relationship. My view is that the only reason there are three divisions and three chiefs of the Stoney people is greed. Everyone wants to be a chief, and there is three times the opportunity for greed if there are three chiefs.

Ernest Wesley did do one great thing during his second tenure as chief, however, and that was to hire Yvonne DePeel as superintendent of the Stoney Education Authority.

Yvonne is an attractive woman, of medium height and a slim build, her hair is blond and her eyes seem to change colour from green to blue depending on the light and the surrounding colours. Far more than her appearance, her attractiveness comes from her dedication to children, her energy, her humour and her enthusiasm. She told me once that she often deliberately plays the dumb blonde because it puts people off guard and makes them easier to deal with (manipulate might be a better word). She can be quite manipulative, and she used this ability to raise millions of dollars for programs and new schools for the Stoney Nakoda First Nation. (I refuse to use the term Stoney Nakoda First Nations.)

Yvonne had been hired after the third-party management had insisted on rules that would separate program management from political interference. She made it a term of her contract that there would be no political interference, and for nine years under her direction the schools had thrived because the old practice of a chief or councillor causing a teacher to be fired because there was difficulty with a favoured child stopped. Those rules may not have worked had someone else been in the position, but Yvonne was strong enough to make sure they were observed. In my view, March 2010 marked the end of this era of progress and a return to John Snow-like tyranny.

Mary Stacey called to tell me about the terminations. Yvonne had gone to Prince Albert to be with her mother and sister and to deal with her own emotional trauma. The loss of her position was devastating for her, and it was the second personal tragedy she had had to deal with. In October 2009 her son, Jordan, had taken his own life. She had taken three months of bereavement leave, and when she came back Greg Varricchio was the new CEO and was demanding control of education and social services. One of Yvonne's concerns was that he wanted control of her funding and she was unwilling to give it. She told me about her concerns. She had applied, in conjunction with the education directors of the Kainai, Piikani and Tsuu T"ina First Nations, for a grant to continue her literacy program at Morley and expand it to these additional three First Nations as well. The grant was from INAC through their Improving Schools Program and it had been approved at $1.6-million. Yvonne said the program was started in January without funding, but when she began making inquiries about it in March she was told the money had in fact been advanced to the Treaty 7 regional management office in December.

She laughed when she told me she felt really stupid when she went to a meeting with the three chiefs and warned them that as directors of Treaty 7 they might be in trouble because this money had gone missing. She said the chiefs reacted strangely to her comments, as if they already knew all about it.

Yvonne asked me to meet with the elders on the education committee because they were upset about what was happening and needed someone to talk to. She said it would be good for them just to know I was concerned. At one of these meetings – supper with Yvonne and a number of the Stoney elders, including John and Helen Wesley from the Niska Waptan (Big Horn) reserve near Nordegg – they talked of building the school at Big Horn. Some 80 band members had gone to Edmonton to tour schools so that they could make decisions on what they would have in their new school. There were elders and children included on the trip. Yvonne had tears in her eyes as she recalled the morning after they arrived. She thought she was an early riser but when she came to breakfast everyone was waiting for her. It was apparent that she wasn't just building a school, she was building a community.

Myrna Powderface, a Stoney woman who has been an activist on the reserve for many years, called me and asked if I would meet with her and a few others who were concerned about the situation. One of these was Myrna's mother, Kathleen Poucette, who had been a member of the education committee. She showed me a letter from the tribe's lawyers, Rae & Co., which read as follows:

Attention Kathleen Poucette
Dear Madam:
Re: Immediate Cease and Desist

Please be advised that we are counsel to the Stoney Nakoda Nations, which includes the Stoney Tribal Administration, the Stoney Chiefs & Councils, and the directors, officers, administrators and agents acting on their behalf (together the "Nation"). We have been advised that, by way of oral statements uttered by yourself, you have been distributing untrue information concerning and bringing into disrepute the Chief Executive Officer of the Stoney Tribal Administration, the Chiefs and Councils of the Stoney Nakoda Nations, and certain agents of the Nation, including Mr. Shawn Marquis, Mr. Trent Blind and Mr. Norm Brennand.

You should be aware that under Alberta law, uttering remarks to third parties that would tend to lower their estimation of a person or organization constitutes defamation, and is actionable. Your actions are particularly grievous in this case as they are malicious, that is to say your remarks were made for the sole purpose of damaging the Nation's reputation in circumstance where you had no legitimate reason for making such remarks.

At present the Nation is deciding whether to pursue these matters through the courts. On behalf of the Nation, we hereby advise you that if you do not cease and desist with respect to your efforts to harm the Nation's reputation, and withdraw all threats you have made, an action may be commenced against you without notice in the Alberta Court of Queen's Bench. Such an action would not only pursue damages but also seek an order restraining you from further contact with any of the Nation's employees, chiefs, councillors and members. Such a restraining order would also bar you from attending the offices of the Stoney Tribal Administration. In the event that this becomes necessary, the Nation will also be seeking an order requiring you to pay its legal costs.

The Nation considers this a most serious matter, and has already advised us that it will take legal steps to protect its reputation and will commence an action against you in the event that your actions continue.

We trust you will govern yourself accordingly.

> Yours truly,
> Rae & Company
> Oliver W. MacLaren
>
> cc: Chiefs and Council of the
> Stoney Nakoda Nation;
> Greg Varricchio,
> Chief Executive Officer,
> Stoney Tribal Administration

I was angered and embarrassed by the letter. I was embarrassed because as a member of the legal profession I saw this letter as nothing more nor less than bullying. I drafted a letter to MacLaren reminding him of his oath of office and telling him that it is one thing for a lawyer to act for a client who has done wrong and to do everything in his power to ameliorate the consequences of that wrongdoing, but it is another thing for a lawyer to assist a client in doing wrong, and that intimidating band members from speaking out against abuses in tribal government might be closer to the latter than the former.

Kathleen, the dear lady, was obviously concerned, and a little frightened, by the letter, but she laughed and said, "If I'm ordered not to talk to any band members, would that mean I can't talk to myself?"

"You know, it seems to me," she continued, "that there is something wrong when the tribal lawyers are threatening to sue me, a band member, on behalf of some white guys that are working for the band, because I'm not happy with what they are doing. I'm a band member and they are using band funds to fight me."

I wholeheartedly agreed with her. I said:

I don't think you have to worry about that letter. I think it's just bullying nonsense. In the first place, truth is a defence. You tell me that Greg Varricchio has fired Yvonne DePeel. I know that Yvonne DePeel has brought the school on this reserve from no graduates nine years ago to 17 graduates this year. I know that she has created a literacy program that is being copied by three other First Nations. I know that she has built one school and obtained funding for another. If I form a negative opinion of him, that doesn't mean you defamed him. He has defamed himself by his actions, and as long as you speak the truth he has no claim against you.

Re Norm Brennand, you tell me he has taken a job with the band, when we know he has been the INAC representative here for years, including the last year. We also know it is contrary to INAC policy for him to take a job within a year of leaving, but he takes it anyway. He knows or should know that good people were terminated in order for him to get the job. He keeps the job in spite of 170 band members signing a petition to get rid of him. Because you have told me all of this, I may think unfavourably of him but you have not committed defamation as long as what you say is true.

The comments you have made to me, a third party, have hugely lowered my estimation of Greg Varricchio and Norm Brennand, but those comments are not actionable defamation if they are true.

Also, it would be highly unlikely that the tribal council would initiate an action against you. If they did, they would be subject to a demand for documents, and examination for discovery. This means they would have to make available to you every document in their possession relating to the firing of Yvonne DePeel and the hiring of Norm Brennand. They would have to disclose all of the money that has been paid out and where it came from. They would also have to produce each of the claimants for examination by your lawyer. This tribal government doesn't want to disclose everything it has been doing, and that's what they would have to do to sue you, so don't worry about it.

I had other meetings with other elders, and the atmosphere of fear and despair was very similar to the dark days of John Snow. It was not surprising for me to learn that the old chief's sons, John Snow Jr. and Tony Snow, were involved, along with Terry Munro, the Reverend Dr. Chief John Snow's "go-fer," who had arranged for Ernest Hunter's perjured statutory declaration to be sent to the chief judge.

John Snow Jr. had run for Wesley council in the 2006 election but was not successful. We speculated that since he couldn't get elected himself, he was probably exercising the powers of chief by manipulating David Bearspaw.

Rob Shotclose, a former band administrator and a member of the Bearspaw division of the Stoney Nation, told me about his concerns regarding Chief David Bearspaw (chief of the Bearspaw division). Shotclose was most concerned about Bearspaw's hiring of Norm Brennand.

Brennand had been hired at a salary, rumoured to be $180,000 a year, that contained a term that, if he were terminated for any reason, he would be paid a full year's salary. Brennand had been working as an INAC representative on the Stoney reserve for a number of years and right up to his recent retirement. It is INAC policy that no one who works for the department may accept employment with any band they have been dealing with as an INAC representative. Brennand was clearly in breach of the rule, but when Shotclose wrote a letter of complaint to INAC they would do nothing about it. A petition demanding Brennand's removal, signed by 170 residents of the Eden Valley reserve, was ignored by both INAC and Chief Bearspaw.

Other people David Bearspaw had reportedly gathered around him as advisers were former Bearspaw chiefs Una Wesley and Philomene Stevens.

Una Wesley had been elected in the 1970s as the first female chief at Morley. I have not been able to find a copy of the case, but it is a matter of oral history that while she was chief she had given a piece of road repair equipment to her brother, Lenny. I believe it was a grader. In any event, the machine was the property of the tribal administration and she was charged with theft from the administration. At trial she pleaded "tribal custom" and called evidence to show that it was an accepted practice in her Aboriginal community that a chief would look after her family and that this justified her action. Wesley was acquitted, and although there doesn't seem to be a report of the case, it nevertheless seems to be the precedent that prevents any charges being laid against chiefs and councillors for whatever moneys or property they take for themselves from tribal revenue.

In my view the case is nonsense. Had the Crown been prepared to meet this defence, it could have called any number of elders who would have refuted the claim. That wasn't done, and the effect is that ordinary band members, deprived of services that are unavailable because of what the chiefs take for themselves, have no protection.

On November 27, 1997, the *Calgary Herald* published an article written by respected elder and former teacher John Robinson Twoyoungmen entitled "Phoney 'tribal custom' decimating Stoneys." Twoyoungmen's article read in part:

> ... there are two conflicting political philosophies, each called tribal custom.
>
> The genuine brand of tribal custom has been passed down to us by our elders and carries the gentle wisdom of centuries of life together in community.
>
> The other is a concoction by government bureaucracy deaf to the true teachings of our elders. This brand elevates control to the level of Almighty God. It has grown to be a manual for corruption and the destruction of human dignity. This is the system that dictates life on our reserve today.

Philomene Stevens was the Bearspaw chief in the darkest days of John Snow's tyranny. An article in the *Herald* on September 15, 1997, "Chief used public funds for nanny," reported that Chief Stevens had used tribal funds to pay $2,000 per month for a nanny for her four daughters for the summer. At the time this was happening, she had a notice posted on her office door telling band members there was no money for food vouchers or unauthorized medical expenses. The *Herald* article also claimed Stevens had collected $1,200 a month from a welfare program called Child out of Parental Home. The program was intended to assist people caring for foster children, but Stevens had no one else's children in her care at the time.

In my view, any public official in any non-Aboriginal community in Canada who was shown to have done this would be prosecuted for a trust theft and would likely be sentenced to a term of imprisonment. Prosecuting people who steal from programs designed to help children protects those children. Not prosecuting such people means the children who need the services do not receive the protection of the law.

The federal government says it respects the independence of Canada's First Nations and will not interfere in their internal affairs. I hear this as the government saying "we will not protect First Nations children who are the victims of trust thefts by First Nations chiefs and councils."

In the discussions I was having with these concerned band members and elders, we speculated on the advice that David Bearspaw would be getting from his retinue. The "Snow boys" had the benefit of their father's expertise in running the reserve as his private fief for many years. It appeared that his sons were now teaching the old tactics to David Bearspaw and manipulating him to their own advantage as well.

We speculated that Una Wesley and Philomene Stevens would be assuring Bearspaw that he could take all the money he wanted and nothing would happen to him. After all, they themselves had been able to do so for years without ever suffering any consequences.

The conjecture about Norm Brennand was that he had been hired in the expectation that he could use his contacts in INAC to gain concessions from the federal department and also to protect them from the possibility of any action being taken against them by INAC.

It also seemed that Brennand's specific job assignment was to keep Bearspaw in power for an extra two years without having an election.

Each of the three so-called First Nations at Morley has a different electoral cycle: the Wesley elects for a four-year term, the Chiniki for three and the Bearspaw for two. This year (2010) should be an election year for the Bearspaw, but Chief Bearspaw's advisers reportedly are holding private interviews with elders in an attempt to declare a consensus that there should be a four-year term.

When Ernest Wesley was chief of the Wesley he extended their term from two years to four by this same questionable method. Most of the elders who spoke to me about it said they thought such a change should be done by a formal referendum as opposed to a private meeting that was then declared a consensus. However, Wesley did it before an election, so he was in fact elected for the four-year term. The fear today is that David Bearspaw intends to change the term and then just stay in office for another two years without the need for an election.

It amuses me to reflect on the days when I publicly condemned the government of Chief John Snow and was told I should respect the "democratically elected" government of the Stoney people. In my view there is no democracy on this reserve. My impression is that reserve elections are decided by payoffs, scare tactics and manipulation. In non-Aboriginal communities these would result in serious charges under the Canada Elections Act. On reserves there is no mechanism for applying and enforcing these provisions, and abuses occur with impunity.

One of the recommendations of the Royal Commission on Aboriginal Peoples was that local communities should not be recognized as First Nations, and that this term should apply only to larger groupings of Aboriginal communities. I believe that if this were done, it would go a long way toward removing the problems of abuse of power. In larger groupings, single families would not be able to dominate, elected officials would have to develop policies that were good for the whole community, and there would be a bigger pool of talent from which to choose leaders.

But while the Royal Commission recognized the advantage of bigger groupings, the Stoneys have moved in the opposite direction. Their small community, now numbering about 4,500, is subdivided into three. As I have said, the only logical explanation for this is greed. It allows three greedy people to be chiefs and 12 more greedy people to be councillors. It reduces the talent pool for every key position, not just in government but in every other area of need on the reserve.

In my work as the local judge, if I determine that an accused person needs counselling for alcohol or drug abuse (and I estimate this is so for about 80 to 90 per cent of the Aboriginal offenders I see), there may or may not be a qualified addictions counsellor available to them, depending on which of the three tribal divisions the person belongs to.

In one of the meetings I attended, an elder gave me a copy of a December 2002 letter from Indian & Northern Affairs Canada to the chiefs and councillors of the Stoney band. The letter was responding to an application to have separate funding for the Bearspaw, Chiniki and Wesley. This was during the term of Ernest Wesley, who, as I have said, became obsessed with dividing the three groups. The letter, signed by Barrie Robb, the Alberta regional director general for INAC, clearly set out the department's position that there is only the one band, the Stoney Band of Indians.

It was the elders' view that there should be just one chief. That is the view of many of the elders who have discussed this with me, and it appears to be in accordance with the position of INAC as stated in that letter. But still the division into three separate "nations" continues.

The problems are so great and so obvious, and some solutions so simple, it seems INAC is only interested in avoiding those problems, despite having the right idea about the Stoneys being a single jurisdiction. For example, I was also shown various letters of complaint and INAC's replies, which can be paraphrased as follows:

> *Re Norm Brennand:* It is unfortunate that Norm Brennand has retired from INAC, but ultimately it was his personal choice to pursue other opportunities, which landed him at the Stoney First Nation. It is completely out of the hands of the department.

> *Re an allegation that the chief was selling cattle for personal gain:* If you remain concerned that the chief is selling band cattle for personal gain, and should you or other band members have documentation to support such allegations, this should be forwarded to the nearest detachment of the RCMP, which has the authority to determine whether an investigation is warranted. INAC does not have the mandate or authority to investigate matters of a criminal nature.

> *Re interference in post-secondary education:* In response to the concerns of your First Nation managing post-secondary funding, you should be aware that it is the department's policy to devolve responsibility for the management of programs and services funded by the department to the First Nation council. The First Nation council then makes decisions and establishes guidelines and policies to meet the needs of the community. Therefore, I would encourage you as a member of the Stoney First Nation to address your concerns in writing to your elected officials regarding post-secondary education practices and policies.

I had spent years in my own struggle with Chief Judge Wachowich and Chief Judge Walter because they disagreed with my views on Aboriginal justice issues. The conflict had taken its toll on my health and finances and I didn't feel I had the energy to do it again. In short, I was afraid. I was intimidated by the threat of a defamation lawsuit. I am confident that the information I have been receiving is accurate, and I am more than confident there are horrendous violations of the civil rights of band members being committed by the chiefs and councils. However, I also know that the chiefs and councils have unlimited resources for hiring lawyers and prosecuting lawsuits. In 1998 and 1999 I incurred legal expenses in excess of $250,000 in fighting a specious order to transfer me away from the courts where I dealt with Stoney offenders, and a perjured complaint that was engineered by John Snow and his factotum, Terry Munro.

I hadn't sent the letter to Rae & Co. in relation to their bullying of Kathleen Poucette because I didn't want to take direct action that would compromise my ability to continue sitting as a supernumerary judge.

I had been meeting with the elders and others because they asked me to. They trust me because they believe that I speak the truth and that when I do so, people listen. I wanted to give them as much advice and encouragement as I could, but I didn't want to directly involve myself; I didn't want to expose myself to the kind of stuff I had had to deal with in the '90s. But I could not watch their frustration and do nothing. I was hopeful I might be able to get some reaction if I wrote directly to the federal and provincial ministers, who might be able to do something.

So I wrote and forwarded the following letter:

The Honourable
Chuck Strahl,
Minister of Indian &
Northern Affairs
Alberta Region, Canada

The Honourable
Alison Redford,
Minister of Justice &
Attorney General
Alberta, Canada

May 17, 2010

Dear Ministers,

This is to inform you that there are serious abuses occurring on the Stoney Indian reserve at Morley, and to plead with you to act together for the sake of the poor and the children on this reserve.

I address you jointly because I believe you must work together.

My experience in this regard is that I have been the Provincial Court Judge primarily responsible for cases arising on this reserve for most of the last 30 years. In 1997 I ordered the investigation of political corruption and financial mismanagement on this reserve because I became aware of abuses on the reserve that in my view were significant contributing factors to the disproportionate number of criminal offences that came from this community. In 1999 I conducted a fatality inquiry into the suicide of a young Stoney, Sherman Labelle. In that inquiry, I heard witnesses who testified to the chaos in Stoney Child & Family Services and in Education, and I found that these are a major cause of the disproportionate number of suicides of young people in this community.

In 1997 the order captured national media attention and resulted in third-party management being imposed. Human resources rules and accountability rules were established and for ten years there has been reasonably good social order. I believe that the abuses of pre-1997 are being repeated.

In 1997 the then Minister of Justice for Alberta, Jon Havelock, and the then Minister of Indian Affairs, Jane Stewart, both tried to avoid my order by saying it was the responsibility of the other. The fact is that there are abuses which are the responsibility of Indian Affairs, and there are abuses that, if my information is correct, are criminal and therefore the responsibility of the provincial Minister of Justice. Because of this dichotomy, no effective action is taken and the result is that the poor and the children do not have the protection of the law.

What I know is that the three chiefs of the reserve, Cliff Poucette of the Wesley, Bruce Labelle of the Chiniki and David Bearspaw of the Bearspaw, have hired a new CEO, Greg Varricchio, and he has terminated the employment of the Superintendent of Education, Yvonne DePeel, and the Director of Child & Family Services, Carolyn Gordon.

What I believe is that the reason for these terminations was to allow funds in Education and Child & Family Services to be blended with general funds to cover shortfalls in other areas. If these funds are being misapplied, it is in breach of Indian Affairs policy; if they are being paid to the chiefs personally, it is criminal.

I am told that assistance for some 200 special-needs children has been terminated and that the three chiefs paid themselves each $600 for attending the meeting in which they did this. I understand that the chiefs constitute the Child & Family Services Board, and this is in violation of Indian Affairs policy.

One of the stipulations for the removal of the third-party management in 1998 was the separation of program management from political interference. There can be no question that the terminations of Ms. DePeel and Ms. Gordon are breaching this condition. If it is being done so that the chiefs can pay money to themselves, this should be prosecuted as a trust theft.

I am told that $1.6-million was paid by INAC to the Treaty 7 Regional Management Office, pursuant to the Improving Schools Program, to fund the literacy program that Ms. DePeel developed and to provide it to the Tsuu T'ina, Piikani, Kainai and Stoney First Nations. This money was evidently paid by INAC in December 2009 but was not available to the schools until March, and was apparently diverted to other uses in the meantime.

I am told that $16,000 was paid from NNADAP [National Native Alcohol & Drug Abuse Program] moneys for the purchase of a horse for Chief Bearspaw.

The terminations, and the predictably negative impact on Education and Child & Family Services, will predictably cause an increase in crime, suicide and other social dysfunction in this community.

I have suggested to the band members who have pleaded with me to help them that they take their complaints to George Arcand, the Regional Director for INAC. They say he is a "chief's man" and will do nothing to help the common people.

I beg you to take immediate action to stop what is happening. If I can be of any help, you are welcome to contact me.

Yours truly,
John Reilly

I received the following replies, the first one from Alison Redford, the Alberta Minister of Justice and Attorney General:

Dear Judge Reilly:

Thank you for your letter dated May 17, 2010, in which you expressed your concerns regarding conditions on the Stoney Indian reserve at Morley. Unfortunately the issues you identified regarding First Nation governance and financial management fall within the jurisdiction of the Government of Canada.

In your letter you also suggested that some of the activities which you advise have taken place on the reserve may constitute criminal conduct. If you have information concerning suspected criminal activity, I would recommend that you report it to the RCMP in order that the matter can be investigated.

I appreciate that you have taken time to express your concerns.
Yours truly,

(signed)
Alison Redford, QC
Minister

cc: Honourable Chuck Strahl,
Minister of Indian & Northern
Affairs Canada

I should be grateful that Minister Redford at least replied even if she completely missed the point. I know that Indian Affairs is federal. I know that prosecution of offences under the Criminal Code is provincial. That's the problem. I had the naïve hope that Minister Redford might just contact Minister Strahl and suggest that they should have their departments work together to end the corruption that everyone seems to know is rampant on Indian reserves but that nobody does anything about.

To be fair to the provincial minister, given that Indians are federal jurisdiction, it would probably take a joint action by Parliament, all ten provincial legislatures, the three territorial assemblies and 633 First Nations chiefs and councils to even suggest a change in the status quo. The minister may not have felt like taking that on just because the old judge at Morley is fed up with sending Indians to jail because they are the natural product of their environment.

At least Minister Redford replied herself. The response from Indian Affairs didn't even indicate that the minister had seen the letter:

Dear Judge Reilly:

This will acknowledge receipt of your letter dated May 17, 2010.

As per departmental policy on allegations and complaints, I have taken the liberty of forwarding your message to departmental officials in the Alberta Region and to the Audit and Evaluation Office.

The Audit and Evaluation Office have the mandate to review all relevant information and determine if additional measures, up to and including forensic audits, may be appropriate to protect the delivery of the services funded by the Department.

If you want additional information on their mandate or the status of the investigation, please contact Mr. Jean-Jacques Lemay, Director of the Assessment and Investigation Services at:

Jean-Jacques Lemay
Director, Assessment and Investigation Services
Audit and Evaluation Sector
Indian & Northern Affairs Canada
Room 335 – 90 Sparks Street
Ottawa, ON K1A 0H4

Please note that all correspondence received is subject to the provisions of the Access to Information and Privacy Acts.

Sincerely,

(signed)
Marie-Ève Bonneville
Allegations and Complaints
Administrator

These letters were both bureaucratic put-offs. Politicians know the Indian Question is a Pandora's box. They are afraid to open it, so they just ignore it and hope it will continue to go unnoticed until their term of office is over. In the meantime, children like Sherman Labelle are deprived of the services they require, and when the frustration and despair of their lives gets too bad they commit suicide. Elders like Kathleen Poucette do what they can, and mostly just "grin and bear it" as they have done for generations.

As I finish this manuscript, I note that the *Calgary Herald* for June 26, 2010, has an article on page A4 headlined "Canada pledges $1.1B for women's and kids' health": "Prime Minister Stephen Harper emerged from the G8 meeting Friday with a boast that Canada will pay a large share of a multibillion-dollar global plan to improve the health of women and children in poor countries."

While I truly applaud this initiative, I lament the fact that the Prime Minister can have such compassion for women overseas while so many babies right here at home are being born with fetal alcohol syndrome but nobody wants to even admit there is a problem, let alone do anything about it.

As a judge, I'm not supposed to make comments like this, but the words of Edmund Burke keep ringing in my mind. They will not allow me to remain silent: "All that is necessary for the triumph of evil is that good men do nothing."

That worked for John Snow, and it seems to be working for David Bearspaw.

APPENDIX A

[The following is a verbatim copy of the official text as provided by the Alberta Provincial Court, Criminal Division, at Cochrane, Alberta.]

Indexed as:
R. v. Hunter

Between
Her Majesty the Queen, and
Ernest Vernon Hunter

[1997] A.J. No. 723

52 Alta. L.R. (3d) 359

35 W.C.B. (2d) 308

Docket No. 70015995P10101

Alberta Provincial Court - Criminal Division
Cochrane, Alberta

Reilly Prov. Ct. J.

Heard: June 26, 1997.

Oral judgment: June 26, 1997. Filed: July 4, 1997.

(13 pp.)

Counsel:
No counsel mentioned.

JUDGMENT

1   **REILLY PROV. CT. J.** (orally):– The accused in this case has entered a plea of Guilty to a charge of Assault Causing Bodily Harm which involves a serious domestic assault. Given the guidelines in R. v. Brown, Highway and Umphreville, (Alberta Court of Appeal) 125 A.R. 150, the accused fits the circumstances of Highway so closely that a sentence of 18 months would appear to be appropriate.

2   This raises a number of issues that have concerned me for some time. These include the conditions on the reserve at Morley, the futility of imprisonment, the cultural conflict between the Law of Canada and Aboriginal people.

3   Sentencing will therefore not be dealt with today. It will be adjourned to the fall and there will be an Order directing that the Chief Crown Prosecutor, Bruce Fraser, Q.C., cause an investigation into social conditions, political corruption, and financial mismanagement on the Stoney Indian Reserve at Morley and that he produce a report thereon, so that I may properly comply with Section 718.2(e) of the Criminal Code.

4   This subsection reads as follows:

> "(e) all available sanctions other than imprisonment that are reasonable in the circumstances should be considered for all offenders, with particular attention to the circumstances of Aboriginal offenders"

5   I am of the view that this man should not go to prison. In the Highway case reference was made on behalf of the accused to the findings of The Cawsey Report. The court said at page 158:

> "neither a trial court nor an appellate court is likely to be

impressed by some vague reference to cultural differences between Aboriginal communities and non-Aboriginal society unsupported by more."

6   I accept the dictum that vague references are not enough. However, I am convinced that cultural differences are crucial to determining just dispositions. The Court indicated that there might be a difference in sentencing approach if there were programs in the Aboriginal community that could deal with the accused. In my view there are other very important circumstances.

1   The incidence of the offence in the community. If it is so common that it is virtually the norm, it may be a further injustice to punish the accused rather than deal with the underlying social problems.

2   The incidence of prosecution of the offence. If the accused is one of many who have committed the offence, but one of only a few who have been successfully prosecuted, his guilty plea may be a far more important factor in mitigation.

3   The reason that programs that may have helped prevent the offence are not available. Is political corruption and financial mismanagement the reason that there is no funding for programs?

4   The incidence of unprosecuted crime, of which the accused may be a victim. If he is prosecuted but not protected by law, is this justice?

5   Is social dysfunction generally so serious that it is a significant cause of the accused behaviour.

7   Mr. Justice Sopinka makes the following statement in giving the majority judgement of the Supreme Court of Canada in R. v. McDonnell [judgment rendered April 24, 1997, at pg. 10];

"A sentencing judge also possesses the unique qualifications of experience and judgement from having served on the front lines of our criminal justice system. Perhaps most importantly, the sentencing judge will normally preside near or within the community which has suffered the consequences of the offender's crime. As such, the sentencing judge will have a strong sense of the particular blend of sentencing goals that will be 'just and appropriate' for the protection of the community."

8   I have been one of those front line judges for twenty years. For 16 years I sat in Calgary and often came to Cochrane as one of the Calgary judges who did this circuit. Cochrane is now part of the Canmore Court Circuit for which I am the resident judge. Because of the large number of Stoney People who appear here in Cochrane I have been attempting to educate myself in relation to Aboriginal issues, and I believe that section 718.2(e) is a long overdue step towards bringing justice to Aboriginal people.

9   Last year I started a project to improve case flow management here in Cochrane and it has developed into a painful exercise in awareness of social disorder and injustice among the Stoney people. In my attempts to find people who would be interested in participating in a justice committee, victim assistance volunteering, and sentencing circles, I have been told over and over again that people are afraid to participate because of repercussions. This fear, and intimidation and violence, appear to be a dominant part of life on this reserve.

10   I have seen many cases of alleged domestic violence called for trial or preliminary only to have the Crown withdraw the case for lack of witnesses. I see very little follow up in these matters. I am told by Stoney people that the victims are afraid to testify because even if the offender is convicted and imprisoned

the victim will be harassed and punished by his family, and on the reserve she will be without protection.

11   The Stoney Indian Reserve at Morley is a community of about 3000 people, divided into three First Nations, the Wesley, the Bearspaw, and the Chiniki. It has been one of the richest reserves in Alberta enjoying oil and gas revenues as high as sixty million dollars in the seventies when its population was only 1500 people. Residents have their houses supplied to them by the Tribal Administration and their utilities are paid out of the oil and gas revenues which are now about nine million a year.

12   Residents of the reserve have described it to me as a 'prison without bars,' and a 'welfare ghetto.' I am told that it has the highest number of suicides, the highest number of children in care, and the highest number of prescription drug addicts of any reserve in Canada. The 'paid for' housing and utilities create a security which most are afraid to leave, but beyond that unemployment is over 90%.

13   The 'ghetto mentality' is an attitude of hopelessness in which people are resigned to the fact that there will never be enough for everyone and survival requires getting enough for yourself, no matter what the cost to others. There is a powerlessness that results in weak people dominating weaker people as the only way that they can feel any sense of self worth. This results in family violence, school violence, and violence in the community.

14   For many years I have been asking why it is that this reserve which should be so prosperous has so many poor people, has such a low level of education, has such horrendous social problems, and has such an apparent lack of programs to deal with those problems.

15   Since trying to get justice programs started myself I have

at least found people who will explain the problem to me, and the explanations include allegations of political corruption that one would associate with the dictatorship of a banana republic.

16   I have asked Mr. Fraser to appoint a permanent prosecutor for the court here in Cochrane, not for the better prosecution of Stoney offenders but for the better protection of Stoney victims.

17   If there were one prosecutor he could study the conditions at Morley so that he could give attention to matters that require attention. He would also be in a position to advise the court on the circumstances of offenders that are relevant in sentencing. Cases here are prosecuted by any one of a team of nine prosecutors which means a different prosecutor at almost every court sitting and none of them with any special knowledge of conditions at Morley. As long as this situation prevails, I find that the only way I can comply with the law as stated in section 718.2(e) is to order this investigation.

18   Over and over, in the conversations I have with Stoney people and non-Stoney who have worked on the reserve, the finger is pointed at Chief John Snow as a significant factor. If the allegations which I will now set out are shown to be false, I will most humbly apologize to Chief Snow. If they are true, he is guilty of a self-interest and exploitation of his people that is unbelievable for a so-called democratic community lying between the great City of Calgary and the beautiful Rocky Mountains.

19   He is only one of three chiefs, but being first elected in 1969, and remaining chief until now with the exception of 1992 to 1996, he has dominated the political scene at Morley for most of the last thirty years.

20   He has two Honorary Doctorates and is given credit for writing the book *These Mountains Are Our Sacred Places*. He is an ordained United Church Minister and has recently served as head of the All Tribes Presbytery of United Church for all reserves in Alberta.

21   He speaks of improving the lot of his people but during his years as chief there appear to be no responsible positions filled by Stoney People and no lasting programs. In 1991 he fired 17 teachers at the Morley Community School and there are still outstanding law suits against the Stoney Educational Authority for wrongful dismissals. I am told that since his return to power in 1996 the employment of over 80 people has been terminated, 80% of them are Stoney. Among those laid off are all of the members of the Stoney Tribal Police, the school principal, Allen Elkin, and the vice-principal, Mary Anna Harbeck, and just this week the acting principal, Janet Embacher.

22   I am told that the school has an enrolment of about 650, but that attendance is about 250, and that the reason for the absenteeism is largely bullying and intimidation. In this community where there is so much instability and where a continuity of teachers would seem to be so important it is mystifying that a chief who is concerned about his people would create instability at the school with these firings. The explanation that is given to me is that he deliberately interferes with Stoney education because the less educated his people are, the more he is able to dominate them.

23   I am told he did not send his children to the school at Morley, but used his position as Chief to have a separate school bus take them to Springbank Community School.

24   I have attended the Nakoda Lodge on a number of

occasions. This lodge is the an enterprise owned by the Wesley First Nation, but I am advised that Snow uses it as his personal business. I am told that he and his extended family use the facilities without paying and most of their food is obtained by taking it from the lodge. I am also informed that he freely uses the receipts as his own income. It was reported in the Canmore paper shortly after the election last year that the Federal Government had made a grant of $100,000.00 for improvements to the Lodge. With tourism the most profitable industry in the Bow Valley it may be a very serious indication of his self interest and lack of concern for his people that he gets money for this and not for the badly needed programs to deal with social problems. It may also be a matter of interest to Canadian taxpayers that the Government pays money for what should be a profitable business on its own.

25   I have seen hundreds of logging trucks taking logs off of the Reserve. I am told that the value of logs removed is about fifty million dollars. Chief Snow publicly criticizes the logging but I am informed that he was doing it himself, and there is a suspicion that he received large sums of money from logging firms to help him win the election, and that one of his first acts as Chief was to discontinue law suits started by the former administration to recover stumpage fees on behalf of the Stoney First Nations from those that were logging. I am told that one of the defendants was Philomene Stevens, now the Chief of the Bearspaw First Nation. My understanding is that the title to the lands that comprise the Stoney Indian Reserve is in the name of Her Majesty the Queen in trust for the Stoney People, and that all of the resources on that land are the common property of all of the people. It seems to me that if individual Stoney people were selling timber to logging companies they were in fact stealing it from their community, and the companies that were buying it were buying stolen

property. If nothing is being done about this exploitation of the Stoney people due to the self interest of their chiefs it is a matter that should be being investigated by the Federal or Provincial Crown.

26   I have attended the Administration Building in Morley for the purpose of assessing the possibility of having a Court sitting there. I have been shown the Council Chamber and told that it is never used by the Chiefs and Council because there are too many people who come there begging for favours from their elected representatives. I am told that all meetings are held in hotels off of the reserve, and some in places as far away as Nevada and Arizona.

27   I am told the misappropriation of funds by Aboriginal Chiefs and Councils is accepted practice on many reserves. I am told by Stoney people that the way government works on the reserve is that the candidate with the most relatives wins and then he and his family share the spoils.

28   I am told that the Director of Indian Affairs will do nothing about it because it is an internal matter.

29   Ordinary Stoney people accept it because it is the way it has always been.

30   My understanding of the Law of Canada is that those who hold public office and who use public funds for their own use are committing the criminal act of theft, and it is theft whether or not the victims accept it and whether or not they complain about it. Some of the victims are infant children who don't have milk and clean diapers because their parents are not among the favoured families. Some of the victims are those in need of social programs and for whom there are no programs because funds therefore are not available. The accused in this case says he was doing well on a program and re-offended when funding for the program was discontinued.

31   In my view it is my duty to know what the circumstances in relation to the funding are.

32   These are the questions that I wish answered.

33   With regard to domestic abuse I ask for a review of all files relating to domestic abuse on the Stoney Indian Reserve at Morley and that I be provided with the following information:

1   Over a two year period commencing January 1, 1994, (or whatever date is convenient) how many complaints have been received by the Stoney Tribal Police and the Cochrane R.C.M.P. in relation to domestic abuse?

2   How many of those Complaints have resulted in charges being laid?

3   How many of the charges resulted in pleas of Guilty, and how many were set for Trial or Preliminary?

4   How many Trials and Preliminaries proceeded and how many did not proceed because of lack of witnesses?

5   Where witnesses did not show up, what steps were taken to determine why they had not shown up?

6   Where witnesses were afraid to testify, what steps were taken to protect them?

34   With regard to financial abuses which result in lack of funding for needed programs:

7   How much money have the Chiefs and Council received from the Government of Canada, from oil and gas revenues, from other sources? How much has been spent on travel and accommodation since their election

in December of 1996? How much has been misappropriated for personal use?

8   Did Chief Snow use his position to run a separate school bus for his children? Is it true that they went to school off of the reserve?

9   Is it true that the elected representatives of the Stoney People have their meetings off of the reserve in order to avoid the people who elected them?

10   How much does it cost to pay the expenses of the off-reserve meetings?

11   Where does the money come from? Is it the Canadian taxpayer, or is it the Stoney People?

12   Did the ordinary Stoney receive any of the benefits of the logging? Was the logging carried on according to law? Has anything been done by the Federal or Provincial Departments of Justice to determine these things?

35   With regard to social disorder generally:

13   How many people have been terminated from their employment? What reasons have been given? What are the qualifications of the replacements?

14   Have the Stoney Tribal Police been laid off? That is the effect on the safety of victims of violence?

15   What is the enrolment situation at the Morley school? What is the incidence of violence? What is being done about it? What is the effect of layoffs on school morale and stability.

16   What is the incidence of drug and alcohol addiction? What programs are available for treatment?

17   What is the incidence of suicide? What is being done about it?

36   It is only when I have the answers to these questions that I will be able to assess the truth of these things and thereby know what are the circumstances of Aboriginal offenders from Morley. When the investigation is completed I will deal with the sentencing in this matter.

REILLY PROV. CT. J.

qp/s/bbd

— End of Request —
Print Request: Current Document: 76
Time Of Request: Wednesday, May 26, 2010 10:22:05

APPENDIX B

[The following is a verbatim copy of the official text as provided by the Alberta Provincial Court, Criminal Division, at Cochrane, Alberta.]

Indexed as:
R. v. Hunter

Between
Her Majesty the Queen, and
Ernest Vernon Hunter

[1997] A.J. No. 1215

211 A.R. 110

36 W.C.B. (2d) 495

Docket No. 70015995P10101

Alberta Provincial Court
Cochrane, Alberta

Reilly Prov. Ct. J.

Judgment: filed November 28, 1997.

Statutes, Regulations and Rules Cited:

Criminal Code, ss. 718(a), 718(b), 718(c), 718(d), 718(e), 718(f), 718.1, 718.2(a)(i), 718.2(a)(ii), 718.2(b), 718.2(c), 718.2(d), 718.2(e), 723(3), 723(4), 723(5).

Criminal law – Sentencing – Considerations on imposing sentence – Native people – Uniqueness of community where offence committed.

This was the sentencing portion of the accused's trial on a charge of assault. The accused and his wife were status Indians living on a reserve. The accused pleaded guilty to the assault on his common-law wife. Both the accused and the victim were drinking heavily on the night the assault occurred at a party. The accused had enrolled in an anger management course in Calgary subsequent to the assault, but was unable to complete it because financing from the Band was discontinued. Pursuant to section 718.2(e) of the Criminal Code which provided that sentencing courts were required to pay particular attention to the circumstances of Aboriginal offenders, the court ordered an investigation into conditions on the reserve, including rumoured abuses of power by the Tribal Government.

HELD: The accused was given a suspended sentence for two years with probation. The terms of probation included a requirement that he attend treatment for alcohol abuse and anger management, and perform 100 hours of community service. Respect for the law generally, with particular regard to Aboriginal considerations, did not demand imprisonment and was better met by a treatment-oriented sentence. The most important sentencing consideration in this case was rehabilitation of the accused, particularly because the accused was Aboriginal. The current difficulties faced by many Aboriginal people had their roots in an unfortunate and shameful part of Canada's history. The fact that the victim was the accused's common law spouse was an aggravating factor. The accused had a lengthy record which established an ongoing problem with alcoholism which needed to be addressed. The guilty plea was a mitigating factor. The degree of hopelessness on the reserve, where every aspect of life was controlled by bureaucratic officials, and where nothing would be done for you if you were not connected, was also relevant.

Counsel:

P. Roginsky, for the Crown.

J. Ogle, Q.C., for the defence.

Sentencing Decision

REILLY PROV. CT. J.:–

Introduction

1   In determining what I find to be fit sentence in this matter I have attempted to fully explore the meaning of the phrase "particular attention to the circumstances of Aboriginal offenders" which appear in section 718.2(e) of the Criminal Code.

2   In doing so I have experienced a frustration which I can only imagine to be a faint shadow of the frustration which marks the lives of many of the people who live on the Stoney Indian Reserve at Morley.

3   As I have not followed the guidelines set out by the Court of Appeal I will set out my reasons in detail so that they can be fully reviewed.

The Facts

4   On May 27, 1997 the accused pled guilty to a charge that:

On or about the 1st day of January 1997, at or near Morley, Alberta, did in committing an assault, cause bodily harm to Rondi Lefthand,

5   The particulars were that the accused and his common-law wife were at a party at a residence in Morley. There was an argument that turned into a physical fight. The accused kicked the victim in the head and body while wearing footwear. The victim suffered cuts and bruising on her head, bruising to her ribs and body. Her face was swollen to the point that she wasn't recognizable. On the hearing date of May 27, the victim indicated that she was still experiencing some numbness on her face as a result of the assault.

6   In submissions as to sentence Mr. Ogle said two things that I found to be of significance. One was that the accused had taken a 28 day treatment program in 1995, had subsequently lived in Calgary with the victim and they were staying away from alcohol until returning to the reserve in late 1996. After that both began drinking heavily and that culminated in the incident before the court. This, in my view, raised the question of conditions on the reserve as they relate to alcoholism.

7   The second thing was that the accused, subsequent to the incident had enrolled in an Anger Management Course through Calgary Counselling Services but was unable to complete it because financing from the band, that was necessary for him to stay in Calgary to do the course, was discontinued. This, in my view, raised the question of Tribal finances generally. This was of special concern to me because since the Tribal election of December 1996, I had heard many stories on the reserve of the misappropriation of band funds, and it was my view that if this was in fact occurring it was a relevant circumstance of this Aboriginal accused as it was having a direct effect on his ability to get needed treatment.

The Procedure

8   I set the matter over to June 26, 1997 and ordered a

pre-sentence report. In the meantime, I continued to hear stories of serious abuses of power by the Tribal Government and it was my view that these matters were relevant to the matter before me as conditions on the reserve contribute to the incidence of alcoholism and violence which were a factor in this offence.

9   I therefore ordered an investigation in order to have the particulars of these conditions before me as part of what I should be considering in relation to "circumstances of the Aboriginal accused."

10   There is no question that in making this order I had an expectation that an investigation into the matters I raised might result in charges being laid for any criminal offences that might be uncovered, but I was at all times clear that any such action was the purview of other stake holders in the Criminal Justice System, and that had no function in that regard.

11   My order was appealed to the Court of Queen's Bench by way of an application for certiorari, and Mr. Justice LoVecchio reduced the scope of the order. In doing so Mr. Justice LoVecchio commented on the fact that I read from a prepared text. I see this to be a criticism of my procedure and I accept it as a valid criticism.

12   I did not refer specifically to section 723(3) in making the order, although it was on the basis of that section that my order was partially upheld. With the benefit of hindsight I would have proceeded differently and will proceed differently in future should I have occasion to invoke this section.

13   The subsection reads:

> 723(3) The court may, on its own motion, after hearing argument from the prosecutor and the offender, require

the production of evidence that would assist it in determining the appropriate sentence.

14   On consideration, I believe that the section contemplates that I would make the motion, that is advise the parties of my intention, and then hear any argument that they might have on the motion before requiring the further evidence. Had this been done the matter might have proceeded in a less contentious fashion, and the end result may have been more satisfactory.

15   When I received Ex 5, The Report, I found the results inconclusive and considered the provisions of Section 723(4) as a way of clarifying the information. This subsection reads:

> 723(4) Where it is necessary in the interests of justice, the court may, after consulting the parties, compel the appearance of any person who is a compellable witness to assist the court in determining the appropriate sentence.

16   In view of the fact that the accused pled guilty in May and it was now November, it was my decision that further delays for the purpose of clarifying these corollary matters could not be justified.

Media References

17   I then took the extraordinary step of producing a number of copies of newspaper clippings and requested that counsel allow me the latitude of using these materials as documentation of social and political conditions on the reserve for the court record.

18   Counsel for the defence supported this approach on the basis of section 723(5)

> 723(5) Hearsay evidence is admissible at sentencing

proceedings, but the court may if it considers it necessary in the interests of justice, compel a person to testify ...

19   Crown counsel indicated he was not able to consent, but I took his submissions to not be an objection and entered them as an exhibit. Clearly this material has far too little weight to be used on primary issues before the court, but for the limited purpose of providing general information about the community so that the total picture of the Aboriginal offender's circumstances can be given consideration, and in view of the amount of time that had unfortunately passed in the process of the appeal and production of the inconclusive report, I found this, together with information informally supplied to me personally about the community to be the best evidence available to me.

20   In R. v. McDonnell [judgment rendered April 24, 1997, at p. 10] Mr. Justice Sopinka said:

> Perhaps most importantly, the sentencing judge will normally preside near or within the community which has suffered the consequences of the offender's crime. As such, the sentencing judge will have a strong sense of the particular blend of sentencing goals that will be "just and appropriate for the protection of the community."

21   This statement in my view presumes that a judge will have a knowledge of the community in which he resides and that he will use that knowledge in the sentencing process. I suggest that our general knowledge of our communities comes from what we read in the media, and because of the unique nature of this community, sought to have documentation of these conditions. Again, as I have stated earlier, the newspaper clippings do not directly address the primary issues before me, to wit: an appropriate disposition for the admitted criminal act.

My Knowledge of the Community

22 I have felt some degree of criticism as a result of my somewhat proactive conduct in this matter and therefore wish to address this concern.

23 Judicial independence requires that a judge be free of outside influence in determining matters before him. Undue judicial activism will expose a judge to outside influences and therefore must be approached with caution, and to a large degree avoided. On the other hand, ignorance of the community in which the offence is committed may also be the cause of judicial error, and this has been pointed out many times in relation to Aboriginal offenders. It is my view therefore that I must strive towards achieving a balance in this area.

24 In doing so I believe that I am addressing the problems referred to in The Report of the Task Force on the Criminal Justice System and Its Impact on the Indian and Metis People of Alberta - Justice on Trial (hereinafter referred to as The Cawsey Report):

> "During our visits to Aboriginal communities, we heard the common complaint that judges, prosecutors, lawyers and police never visit Aboriginal communities other than in their official capacities.... There is a very definite perception that judges, prosecutors and lawyers do not know very much about the Aboriginal people with whom they deal. (p. 5.1)

> Judges who are not sensitive to cultural differences and who know little about the community in which they conduct court may well be perceived as judicial tyrants, (p. 5-5)

> The lack of knowledge about Aboriginal people by the legal profession results in the application of a system that

is alien to Aboriginals. The failure of the legal profession to understand this condition results in systemic discrimination. (p. 5-9)

25   In trying to know more about the Stoney people I have come to see the suffering and dysfunction and what I believe to be serious injustice that pervades this community.

26   I am mindful of Mr. Justice LoVecchio's admonition:

> To get at this question by accusing some members of the community of essentially criminal conduct is inappropriate. Those individuals were not before the Court on any charges and they like all citizens are entitled to due process. As I said earlier, it may be that problems exist in this area in the community. If that is so, the responsibility falls to others to investigate and, if appropriate, file charges. That is not the function of a Court.

27   Again I will attempt to strike a balance between respecting this direction and being complete in my pursuit of a thorough examination of the circumstances of this Aboriginal offender.

The Sentence

28   Sentence is suspended for two years with probation, the accused will be of good behaviour and keep the peace, he will attend treatment as arranged for by the Tsuu T'ina/Stoney Corrections Society for alcohol abuse and anger management, he will perform 100 hours of community service work and any work that can be done for the victim will apply as community service.

29   In determining this sentence I have considered each of the following provisions:

> 718. The fundamental purpose of sentencing is to contribute,

along with crime prevention initiatives, to respect for the law and the maintenance of a just, peaceful and safe society by imposing just sanctions that have one or more of the following objectives:

(a) to denounce unlawful conduct;
(b) to deter the offender and other persons from committing offences;
(c) to separate offenders from society, where necessary;
(d) to assist in rehabilitating offenders;
(e) to provide reparations for harm done to victims or to the community; and
(f) to promote a sense of responsibility in offenders, and acknowledgement of the harm done to victims and to the community.

Fundamental Principle

718.1 A sentence must be proportionate to the gravity of the offence end the degree of responsibility of the offender.

Other Sentencing Principles

718.2 A court that imposes a sentence shall also take into consideration the following principles:

(a) a sentence should be increased or reduced to account for any relevant aggravating or mitigating circumstances relating to the offence or the offender, and, without limiting the generality of the foregoing,

   (i) evidence that the offence was motivated by bias, prejudice or hate based on race, national or ethnic origin, language, colour, religion, sex, age, mental or

physical disability, sexual orientation or any other
similar factor,

(ii) evidence that the offender, in committing the
offence, abused the offender's spouse or child
shall be deemed to be aggravating circumstances:

(b) a sentence should be similar to sentences imposed on
similar offenders for similar offences committed in
similar circumstances;

(c) an offender should not be deprived of liberty, if less
restrictive sanctions may be appropriate in the circumstances; and

(d) all available sanctions other than imprisonment that are
reasonable in the circumstances should be considered
for all offenders, with particular attention to the circumstances of Aboriginal offenders.

Respect for the Law

30   The Crown argues that the words 'respect for the law' in
the preamble to section 718 require a jail sentence because of the
seriousness of the offence.

31   It is my view that this is not so. If these words are considered with the rest of the phrase 'and the maintenance of a
just, peaceful and safe society' I believe that respect for the law
will come from sanctions which are most likely to achieve this
purpose.

32   Ex. 3, The report, p. 10, states:

"What is known, is that the incidents of drug and alcohol
abuse are the result of deeper underlying problems in First
Nation communities."

33   There are frequent references in this regard to 'low self-esteem' being a significant factor. So given the fact that the accused in this case is said (by the victim) to be a good person when he is not drinking, I find that sending him to jail will only contribute to the low self esteem and frustration which I believe to be underlying problems. Treatment oriented sanctions on the other hand may be able to assist him in dealing with those problems, controlling his alcoholism and anger and thereby realize a real possibility of reducing his propensity to commit this type of offence.

34   From the Aboriginal perspective this is especially so. There is a basic difference in our Euro-Canadian concept of justice and that of most First Nations. Rupert Ross quotes this paragraph from a justice proposal prepared in 1989 by the Sandy Lake First Nation and in both of his books. (Dancing With a Ghost p. 168, Returning to the Teachings, p. 5)

> "Probably one of the most serious gaps in the system is the different perception of wrongdoing and how to best treat it. In the non-Indian community, committing a crime seems to mean that the individual is a bad person and therefore must be punished ... The Indian communities view a wrongdoing as a misbehaviour which requires teaching or an illness which requires healing.

The Cawsey Report draws these distinctions:

> Justice and dispute resolution in White society can best be illustrated by a retributive model of justice which includes the following:

> Crime is a violation of the state.
>   The focus is on establishing blame or guilt.

Truth is best found through an adversarial relationship between the offender and the state.

Punishment deters and prevents.

Justice is defined by intent and process (right rules)

Community does not play a leading role.

Action revolves around the offender.

Accountability of the offender is put in terms of punishment.

Offences are strictly legal and devoid of moral, social, political and economic considerations.

Past behaviour is an important factor.

Social stigma of criminal behaviour is almost unremovable.

Remorse, restitution, and forgiveness are not important factors.

Offenders play a passive role depending on proxy professionals.

Justice and dispute resolution in traditional Aboriginal societies can be illustrated by a restorative model of justice which includes the following:

Crime is a violation of one person by another.

The focus is on problem-solving and restoration of harmony.

Dialogue and negotiation are normative.

Restitution and reconciliation are used as a means of restoration.

Justice is right relationship and harmony.

The community acts as a facilitator in the restorative process.

The offender is impressed with the impact of his action on the total order.

The holistic context of an offence is taken into consideration including moral, social economic, political and religious considerations.

Stigma of offences is removable through conformity.

Remorse, repentance and forgiveness are important factors.

Offenders take an active role in the restorative process. (p. 9.6)

35   The Cawsey Report also says this:

Rupert Ross captures the attitude of Indians toward the criminal justice system when he observes that the function of the Indian dispute resolution system is to arrive at real resolutions of disputes. Resolution is achieved when the disputive parties return to peaceful co-existence and bad feelings are eliminated. According to Ross, Indians expected the "white" man's system to do the same. Having realized that the criminal justice system does not aspire to the restoring of friendship and harmony, Indians now want the system removed from their communities ..." (The Cawsey Report p. 5.2)

36   There are other statements in The Cawsey Report which I suggest deal with respect for the law:

It is clear that Aboriginal People do not feel that their views are being considered adequately or that these views are applied in Alberta courts. To them the "white" justice system is partial and unfair. Aboriginal culture is not reflected or appreciated in the "white" system of justice. (p. 4-2)

There is ample statistical evidence to suggest that the Canadian Criminal justice system is failing Aboriginal People. (p. 4-2)

Aboriginal leaders, Elders, inmates, young offenders and all who come in contact with the criminal justice system experience the process of being shunted through arrest, bail hearings, remand, trial, and incarceration as one that is impersonal, bewildering and confusing.

To many Aboriginals, the criminal justice system is an imposed foreign system of law that is not compatible with their way of life. It has no respect for the Aboriginal world view. (p. 4-13)

Aboriginal persons are over represented in federal as well as provincial jails in Alberta. Provincially, Aboriginals make up only 4% of Albertans, and 30% of incarcerated persons. (p. 4-29)

Natives receive lesser sentences when they commit a crime against someone of their own race. In contrast non-Natives receive harsher sentences for crimes committed against members of their own race. This inconsistent treatment tends to undervalue Natives as people. (p. 4-31)

... a statistical analysis of court sentencing practices in Alberta and elsewhere in Canada shows that Alberta has the second highest rate of sentenced admissions per 1,000 adults charged in Canada. The figure is 51.5% higher than the National average. (p. 4-33)

The Royal Commission Justice Report makes this statement:

"All the evidence before the Commission makes it clear that the non-Aboriginal justice system has failed the Aboriginal people." (p. 281)

37   It is therefore my conclusion that respect for the law generally, and with particular regard to Aboriginal considerations,

does not demand imprisonment and is better met by a treatment oriented sentence.

Denunciation

38   There is no question that domestic violence is the worst form of violence. A woman should be able to look to her husband for comfort and protection and when he commits a crime of violence against her he not only violates a sacred trust but he destroys the very fabric of our civilization.

39   This does not mean that imprisonment is the only way that it can be denounced. The above statement and these proceedings, especially having regard to the national attention that this case has received, have denounced the accused's offence.

Deterrence

40   Deterrence was the primary reason for the sentences in the guideline case of Brown, Highway and Umphreville (Alberta Court of Appeal) 125 A.R. 150. In my view the words of the preamble to Section 718 'one or more of the following objectives' gives a sentencing court the discretion to decide whether or not this (deterrence) should be a primary consideration in the case before it. In my view in all the circumstances of the matter before me, it should not.

41   General deterrence presumes that would-be offenders will be cognizant of likely penalties and will therefore refrain from the behaviour in order to avoid those penalties. With respect to specific deterrence, in this case the offence was committed in an alcoholic rage and it is highly unlikely the harshest of penalties would have had any effect on the accused because it is unlikely that he was thinking about consequences at the time.

42   In relation to the concept of deterrence I quote the following:

> Statistics of recidivism lead us to the inescapable conclusion that sentencing practices and the manner in which sentences are implemented have every little impact on reducing the level of crime in Aboriginal communities ... (The Cawsey Report p. 6-1)

> In many cases, incarceration was not an imposition and, more often than not, it was little deterrence to further criminal activity. (The Cawsey Report p. 6-1)

> Removal to an outside jail ... permits an offender to escape being held accountable to the community. (Quote from Rupert Ross by The Royal Commission Justice Report p. 68)

With respect, in my view, "general deterrence" sentencing in relation to alcohol-based criminal conduct by Aboriginal offenders will not be effective.

Separate Offenders from Society

43   The mitigating factors of alcoholism and other illness will not save an accused from imprisonment if he continues to be a danger to society. Where the accused however has demonstrated a willingness to take treatment and that it can be successful, as in this case, I find that his separation from society is not required.

Rehabilitation of the Accused

44   I find this to be the most important consideration in this case, and especially because the accused is an Aboriginal. The current difficulties faced by many Aboriginal people have their roots in an unfortunate and shameful part of Canada's history. As a judge whose power comes from the dominant society [I] find that in order to do justice to Aboriginal people I must be mindful of the injustices that have been done to these people by the dominant society. I will deal with this in detail under the heading of Historical circumstances.

Reparation to Victim and Society

45   Many offenders when they have done time in prison will say that they have paid their debt to society. I find this to be a contradiction in terms. Keeping these people in prison has simply cost society the price of their keep. Imprisonment does not achieve this goal.

46   I find reparation to be important and have therefore ordered community service. I had no specific recommendations as to how reparation could be made to the victim, so I directed 100 hours of community service work with the provision that if he could do work for the benefit of the victim that would apply as community service. I have followed a practice of making 100 hours the maximum because I have been advised by corrections personnel that any more than this makes supervision unworkable, so this in my view was a maximum number of hours.

Responsibility and Acknowledgement of Harm Done

47   The pre-sentence report says he has accepted responsibility and expressed shame and remorse. He is presently living in a situation that is supportive of a sober lifestyle.

Degree of Responsibility

48   This phrase in section 718.1 indicates a changing attitude in criminal responsibility. It used to be that an accused was either responsible or he was not, but the concept of diminished responsibility was not recognized. The Code now recognizes it.

49   Given that alcoholism is recognized as a result of deeper underlying problems of First Nation Communities, it is my view that we must look at the causes of those underlying problems and accept a collective responsibility for them and therefore a collective responsibility for the offence. To simply imprison the accused because he has succumbed to circumstances that we have helped to create, and which we are doing little to change, is further injustice.

Aggravating Circumstances

50   I find that 718.2(a)(i) does not have application in this case, and I wish to confirm that this violent beating did not involve hatred. It also did not involve vengeance and I am of the view that it did not involve deliberate cruelty. I do not have professional, psychological evidence before me, but I believe that this was an irrational, alcoholic rage, that occurred when the frustration and desperation of the accused's life reached a breaking point. I believe it to be a symptom of that frustration and desperation in the same way that the suicides among the young people in this community are a symptom.

51   718.2(a)(ii) applies and there is no doubt that the fact that the victim was the accused's common law spouse is an aggravating factor in this case.

The Accused's Record

52   The accused has a lengthy record. The law in this regard is that he should not be punished again for that which he has already been punished, but prior leniency may disentitle him to further leniency. My view of his record is that it establishes an ongoing problem with alcoholism which needs to be addressed.

Mitigating Circumstances

Guilty Plea and likelihood of conviction

53   Section 718.2 does not specifically deal with the mitigating nature of a guilty plea, but this has long been accepted by the courts, and the phrase 'without limiting the generality of the foregoing' leaves this unchanged.

54   It is my view that many courts may refer to the guilty plea in mitigation without appreciating how significant it is.

55   I asked the first 5 questions in the Order because it was my overall impression that there were a great many cases of domestic abuse, that there were very few guilty pleas, fewer convictions, and great difficulty with witnesses.

56   The Crown argues that the report was not sufficient to allow any definite conclusions. I acknowledge that I placed the Crown in an embarrassing position by asking these questions. One of my frustrations in dealing with the case load at Cochrane is that there is a very significant problem with the disproportionate number of Stoney people who appear there. (I estimate the population base of this court to be about 20,000 people, the Stoney at Morley are less than 3,000 of these, so they make up roughly 15% of the population and I estimate about 75% of the work of this court). The practice of the Crown Prosecutor's office is to send any one of a group of nine to do the work on any given day. The result is that none of them have any special knowledge of what I regard to be a special problem. I make no criticism of any individual prosecutor, but I believe that this lack of continuity results in a very poor delivery of justice to the Stoney people.

57   The survey shows that out of 42 charges laid in the last two years, there has been one conviction so far, and four guilty pleas. Of ten charges disposed of 5 were dismissed for witness problems, and three found not guilty. From my experience, these numbers appeared to be low. I surmise that this is because the

survey dealt with cases that were commenced in the last two years, and during that time I have been dealing with cases that were commenced more than two years ago. Admittedly, this is a poor statistical base, but the fact is that to date, guilty pleas are one out of ten, and there has only been 1 conviction. Therefore, in assessing the weight to be given to a guilty plea, I find it has great weight, enough to virtually preclude imprisonment unless it is shown to be necessary for the safety of the public.

58   The Crown argued that general problems with witnesses did not apply in this case because they had their witness for the day of trial. My experience is that it would not be a typical for that witness to take the stand and then say that she didn't remember what happened because she was too drunk.

Guilty Plea and What It Saves a Witness

59   Besides the very real possibility of avoiding conviction which an accused gives up when he pleads guilty, the other mitigating feature of his plea is the trauma that he saves the witness. Again, I do not believe that some courts appreciate how important this is when dealing with Aboriginal witnesses.

60   I have seen many Stoney women take the witness stand and appear so afraid and so miserable that I truly believe they would prefer another beating to testifying about the one that is the subject of the hearing. I do not pretend to understand all of the cultural and historical reasons for their difficulties but I will set out as much as I am able to do.

61   1. Fear of Repercussions. This is the most obvious. If she testifies and he is not convicted she may be beaten immediately. If he is convicted and imprisoned he will eventually return from prison, possibly more angry and bitter than when he went and then she will be in more danger. If he is imprisoned his family may well harass her or punish her for her testimony.

62   2. Cultural ethics. There are powerful inhibitions in Aboriginal tradition which relate to non-interference, non-criticism, not expressing anger. Publicly condemning a person, as a witness is required to do in our adversarial system, may well be considered an immoral act which our system is forcing her to commit.

63   3. Community pride. The Stoney are a proud people and she may have great difficulty speaking about matters which bring shame to the whole community.

64   4. Fear of Bad Spirits. In traditional belief people are seen to do bad things because of influence of bad spirits. A direct confrontation with a wrong doer is believed to invite the risk that those spirits will turn their attention to the confronter.

65   5. Fear of Bad Medicine. This is an area which I hesitate to mention but I believe it to be an important factor. The majority of Stoney people at Morley speak English as a second language. The traditions of spirituality and traditional medicine are said to very strong, but they are also a subject of secretiveness. While [I] know little about them I am satisfied that they have a very strong influence. I have seen the fear that people feel when they believe they might be the object of bad medicine, and many carry 'medicine pouches' and other forms of 'protection.' I believe that many witnesses are subject to the fear that bad medicine may be used to punish them.

66   6. Fear of being alone. There is much isolation on the reserve. Many houses are situated so you cannot see one house from another. In this situation it is more frightening for some women to be alone than it is to be with the man who occasionally

beats them. The maxim, "Better the devil you know, than the devil you don't" seems to have a very real application.

67   7. Fear of fines. If the proceedings result in the accused being convicted and fined the witness will also suffer from the hardship occasioned thereby.

68   8. Lack of confidence in the legal system. Both The Cawsey Report and the Royal Commission on Aboriginal Peoples speak of how the legal system has failed the Aboriginal people. I am sure that many, perhaps most, Aboriginal witnesses feel this and all of the other fears they experience in taking the witness stand are aggravated by the feeling that the system doesn't work for them anyway.

69   9. Lack of relationship. To many Aboriginal people, relationship is of paramount importance. In our Euro-Canadian justice system objectivity and impartiality requires a complete lack of relationship between the judge and the accused. This is probably one of the most serious difficulties that Aboriginal people have with the system, because they generally believe that those who are going to have a serious impact on their lives should know something about them.

70   I have seen cases called for trial where the prosecutor will address the courtroom to ask if the witness is present and will then tell the witness to take the stand. Apparently the prosecutor and the witness have never met, and now without establishing any relationship with her, he is going to ask her to do what might be the most difficult and frightening thing in her life. This often results in the witness failing to give any evidence at all.

71   When I consider all of these things, I find that the weight that should be given to a guilty plea is such that it should virtually preclude imprisonment as a penalty.

Circumstances of Aboriginal Accused

72   It is my view that this phrase must include a consideration of social, political, historical and cultural factors which play a role in the commission of offences by Aboriginals and contribute to the special difficulties that they experience in appearing before our courts.

73   It would be unworkable to attempt this in-depth analysis in every case, but it has been of special interest to me since the court in Cochrane became a part of the court circuit for which I am the resident judge. I propose to set out as detailed an analysis as possible so that it can be fully reviewed and hopefully be a useful reference in this area.

Social Circumstances

74   The Stoney Indian reserve at Morley is a community of about 2700 people. They live in rural residences spread over a 650 square kilometre reserve. Their housing is paid for by the Tribal Administration, but many houses are inadequately maintained. While free housing may seem to be an advantage, it has the significant disadvantage of creating a dependency which leaves many Stoney people stuck without adequate facilities and without opportunity to improve their situation.

75   There is a community high school at the Morley townsite on highway 133x, and also a continuing education facility, but the average level of education is said to be lower than other reserves in Southern Alberta, and much lower than the average for the Province.

76   The incidence of unemployment is 37.3% according to Statistics Canada as quoted by Dave LaVallie (Ex 4, The Report, p. 15) In a meeting which was held in March of this year with approximately 30 people in the justice system and the three Stoney Chiefs, Chief Holloway put it at 90%.

77 The incidence of violence is high. Ex 4, The Report, p. 3; 269 assaults reported in a two year period.

78 The incidence of alcohol abuse is high. 65% of the prisoners in Cochrane in a two year period were from Morley, and 76% were arrested for intoxication with no charges. (Ex 4, The Report, p. 3) Presumably, there were also arrests involving alcohol which did result in charges, so it was more than 76% of the arrests that involved alcohol.

79 There is a high incidence of unnatural death and suicide. The report says 2 suicides and 8 other unnatural deaths this year to October 30. The total of unnatural deaths in a two year period was 27 (8 suicides) in a population of about 2700.

80 There is a high incidence of prescription drug abuse.

81 I find that it is fair to say that this is a very dysfunctional community and that this dysfunction is a contributing factor to the commission of the offence of the accused.

Political Circumstances

82 This is the area in which I must be mindful of Justice LoVecchio's admonition, and will restrict my comments accordingly. Since the questions regarding employment were allowed, and the Stoney Tribal Administration has refused to answer them, I will refer to the materials in Ex 5 as the best evidence I have to make findings in this area.

83 Exhibit 5, p. 11, Alberta Report July 14, 1997:

> In all, Chief Snow has laid off over 90 people since his re-election, estimates Mrs. Wesley. "Whole families were fired," charges another source, including the members of the Stoney Tribal Police Force. Currently, four of Chief

Snow's children hold senior posts within the band and two got theirs after the election – Rachel Snow in education and Gloria Snow, who was crowned Miss Indian World in 1993, in social services.

Chief Snow, who excused himself five minutes into an interview with this magazine last week, insists he has done nothing wrong. "There's no truth to them," he says, referring to Judge Reilly's accusations. As for the firings, he explains that "we couldn't meet the payroll in March and had to let some people go." He says the previous administration left the books in a mess. The band had to finance a $2-million debt and the education department, in particular, was in rough shape. "Creditors have been hounding us since we got in," he says.

84   Yet Jim Fleury, assistant regional director for the Department of Indian and Northern Affairs, reports that audited statements indicate the Stoney tribe ran a surplus in 1996. It received $19 million in federal grants and $15 million in natural gas royalties, as well as provincial education grants and income from the Nakoda Lodge and the band-owned gas station.

The two largest departments on the reserve are education (currently controlled by Chief Snow as Chairman of the Stoney Educational Authority) and social services controlled by rookie Bearspaw Chief Philomene Stevens). The education bureaucracy, explains another band employee, who declines to be identified, is a convenient place to put people who have been promised jobs. It is said to be common for employees to show up at work, punch the time clock and immediately head home.

The effect of these layoffs is dramatically demonstrated by an article, Ex 5. p. 42, The Calgary Herald, August 23, 1997:

> Abby Dawn Hunter had achieved her dream of learning how to help others fight the demons that ultimately took her life late Wednesday night.
>
> Hunter, 28, graduated last December as a life skills coach and counsellor on the Stoney reserve, but never got a chance to work.
>
> She was fired along with 39 other band employees last January by Chief Snow after he won a bitter election in December....
>
> Hunter was struck by a car Thursday on Highway 1A about six kilometres west of Cochrane. Police said she was lying on the road, but have not ruled whether it was an accident or a suicide. Alcohol was a factor, according to RCMP.

The unfairness of these firings is demonstrated by an article Ex 5. p. 54, The Calgary Herald, September 27, 1997:

> Staff at the financially troubled Stoney Nation reserve collected welfare payments at the same time as they drew salaries from the band's social services department. Tribal documents collected during a Herald investigation show at least four band members took the payments even as their department built an ever growing deficit, which may top 1.2 million this year.
>
> The department's responsibility is to distribute basic needs to band members with no income, and officials with Indian Affairs confirmed to the Herald that the double payments contravene federal and band regulations.

Other social services alerted the federal Department of Indian Affairs to a "major crisis" developing in Stoney social services eight months ago, according to a letter dated January 27, 1997. The social services deficit has since grown to $500,000 while hundreds of the band's 3,300 members live in poverty. The reserve is 60 miles west of Calgary.

"You may be the only department to save our social services department" wrote the employees - who were fired within days of writing the letter. (highlighting mine)

85   There is further information on the social services saga, Ex 5, p. 70; The Calgary Herald, October 21, 1997,

The probe into welfare abuse on the Stoney Indian Reserve widened Monday with confirmation one of the band's top social services managers is under investigation.

The Herald last month revealed four other social services employees received welfare while collecting salaries this year.

Tribal Administrator Rick Butler confirmed the department's assistant director Shirley Poucette, 44, is now among those under investigation.

The workers face disciplinary action for collecting welfare while on the band's payroll, Butler said.

There may be firings. There may be suspensions, he added.

Documents show Poucette received $66,000 – tax free – in welfare, wages and expenses between December 1996 and last month.

During that period – when the reserve's social services

department's deficit swelled to at least a half million dollars – records also show Poucette also collected $3,495 in welfare payments.

...

Some Stoneys live on as little as $200 a month welfare, while many complain of poor living conditions and others contend with no heat and running water.

...

She was one of three campaign managers for Chief John Snow during last December's tribal election.

86   Ex. 5, p. 77, The Calgary Herald, November 15, 1997, (the handwritten date of September 15, 1997 which appears in Ex 5 is an error):

A Stoney Reserve chief, who told band members earlier this year there was no money left for food vouchers, collected welfare and used public funds to hire a nanny for her children, band sources say.

Bearspaw Chief Philomene Stevens also led a week long business trip to the Embassy Suites Hotel in Phoenix, Ariz., last February at a cost of $18,000.

Sources say Stevens used Band funds in June to hire a Calgary nanny at a cost of $2,000 per month to look after Stevens's four daughters over the summer.

The nanny, Alice Levesque, said she was hired by the chief for a three month contract that ended in August. Levesque said she was paid $2,000 a month – $1,000 from the Bearspaw Band and $1,000 in bi-monthly cheques from the Tribal Common budget for all three bands.

Stevens collected $3,509 between Dec. 30, 1996 and April 28, 1997 from another welfare program for child care.

87   On November 16, 1997 The Calgary Herald reported that the Stoney Reserve band manager said no action would be taken until the results of a forensic audit expected in the Spring.

88   The above confirm what I understand to be the political situation on the reserve. There appears to be a ruling elite which uses large sums of money for itself and gives jobs on the basis of nepotism and political favouritism. For those who do not belong to the elite, there is little hope of employment and sometimes they are even deprived of basic benefits.

89   This situation appears to be aggravated by indifference on the part of the provincial and federal governments.

90   In the course of this case the provincial Government has, at least publicly, taken no action although the Herald has given names and numbers which are in my view sufficient to be reasonable and probable grounds to believe Criminal offences have been committed.

91   The Alberta Court of Appeal has frequently said that the most aggravated examples of theft are theft of public monies and theft by persons in positions of trust. The Herald prints stories of the theft of welfare, monies by officials of the Stoney welfare department and apparently nothing is done.

92   As to the federal government, the Stoney employees who tried to get assistance from the Department of Indian Affairs were fired and there is no news of anything being done about it. There is the forensic audit, but as far as action on what has been happening there is nothing. Now, the Tribal administrator

is using it to put off anything being done about a chief, the chairman of social services, allegedly taking money from social services.

93   Whatever the truth of these allegations, there can be no doubt that the ordinary Stoney, who has no job, no house or inadequate housing, and is in need of social programs that do not exist, must feel a crushing sense of frustration at his inability to receive any help from any level of government. tribal, provincial or federal.

94   I believe that the degree of hopelessness on this Indian Reserve where every aspect of life is controlled by political and bureaucratic officials, and if you are not 'connected,' apparently nothing is done for you, is beyond the experience of most members of main-stream Canadian society

95   I find this to be a very relevant factor in the frustration, and lack of funding, faced by the accused in this case.

Historical Circumstances

96   I find that as a court which receives its power from the dominant society, [I] should be aware of the injustices this dominant society has visited on the Aboriginal people of Canada. If I am not, I may continue those injustices.

Assimilationist Policies & Colonialism

97   Canada's first Prime Minister, John A. Macdonald, stated that it would be Canada's goal "to do away with the tribal system and assimilate the Indian People in all respects with the inhabitants of the Dominion" (The Report of the Royal Commission on Aboriginal Peoples Volume 1, p. 179),

> "Parliament ... crafted educational systems, social policies and economic development plans designed to extinguish

Aboriginal Rights and assimilate Aboriginal people"
(Volume I, supra p. 179)

"In ... the Indian Acts of 1876 and 1880 the Federal government took for itself the power to mould, unilaterally,
every aspect of life on reserves and to create whatever
infrastructure it deemed necessary to achieve the desired
end – assimilation through enfranchisement and, as a con-
sequence, the eventual disappearance of Indians as distinct
peoples" (Volume I, supra p. 180)

Treaties

98   The fact that the treaties were unfair to the Indians is
something which cannot be disputed. I have taken the following
from the Royal Commission.

"One of the fundamental flaws in the treaty-making process was that only the Crown's version of treaty negotia-
tions and agreements was recorded in accounts of nego-
tiations and in the written texts. Little or no attention
was paid to how First Nations understood the Treaties or
consideration given to the fact that they might have had
a completely different understanding of what had trans-
pired" (Volume I supra p. 176)

"Treaty Commissioners took great care to emphasize the
physical aspects of the "caring relationship" and emphasized that the Indian Nations would benefit from treaties
with the Queen. They were assured that no harm would
come to them as a result of the treaty and that their way of
life would be safeguarded." (Volume I p. 167)

To reassure the Indians, Morris promised: "Understand
me. I do not want to interfere with your hunting and

fishing. I want you to pursue it through the country as you have heretofore done." (Volume 1 p. 169)

(Ed. Note: The Court did not assign a paragraph number 99 to the judgment.)

100 The fact that Morris was making this promise while at the very same time the legislation was already in place that provided for the assimilation of these people suggests a dishonesty and lack of goodwill on the part of the Government of Canada making these treaties.

101 My understanding is that when the Stoney signed Treaty 7 at Blackfoot Crossing in 1877, there was no one in attendance who spoke both English and Stoney (Sioux). All proceedings had to be translated into Cree. History tells us that the Stoney had no concept of the ownership or measurement of land, and the Cree didn't either, so they likely had no understanding of the agreement they were making.

102 There can be no question that the Stoney were at an extreme disadvantage in negotiating and understanding what was happening. They, along with the other Indian Nations, still greatly outnumbered the white population of the prairies and while they might have ultimately been defeated in an armed conflict, it was very much in the interests of the whites to make peace. The Stoney say that it was simply their understanding that they would share the land with their white brothers, but they expected to continue to move freely and hunt their traditional areas.

103 One of the disadvantages which the Stoney have faced over the years is that they were lumped in with their traditional enemies, the Blackfoot, when they signed Treaty 7. This has been overlooked by the Royal Commission, which did not recognize the differences among the Peoples signing this treaty.

"In September 1877, Treaty 7 was made at Blackfoot crossing between the Crown as represented by Commissioner David Laird and the Blood, Blackfoot, Peigan, Sarcee and Stoney Nations of the Blackfoot Confederacy." (Volume 1, supra p. 169)

104 The Stoney are a Sioux speaking nation, the Tsuu T'ina (Sarcee) are a Dene speaking nation, and while Stoney and Tsuu T'ina traded with each other, they were both enemies of the Blackfoot Confederacy.

105 It was not until after the railroad arrived in 1885 that the true effect of the Treaty became evident to them. It was then that the allotment of land was surveyed and then in 1887 they were prohibited from leaving it.

Reserves

106 I often hear non-Aboriginals ask why the Indians don't just leave the reserves if they are so bad. In this regard I think we have to reflect on the fact that they did not ask to be put there in the first place, but after 120 years of knowing nothing else, it is very difficult for them to change. The situation was created by the dominant society and the dominant society owes them something more than just saying they should now deal with it on their own. Justice demands that positive steps be taken to empower them to help themselves, and I see no indication that this is happening.

Residential Schools

"The task force has been told repeatedly of the effect of residential schools on the present generation of Aboriginals. Children were not allowed to wear their own clothing, speak their own language or practice their own customs and traditions. Breaches of the strict codes of discipline resulted in harsh punishments. The boys were not permitted to follow traditional Aboriginal pursuits such as hunting and trapping. ... One of the consequences of residential schooling is that whole generations of Aboriginal children lost their sense of identity as Indian or Metis, including culture, spirituality, and the hunting, trapping, and gathering skills that would have been passed on to them by their parent." (The Cawsey Report p. 8-8)

107 Probably the worst effect of residential schools was the destruction of the Aboriginal families. With their children taken from them there was a vacuum created that many filled with alcohol. There were also generations who grew up without the experience of being in a family situation and they now have no experience of receiving parental care to have as a model for caring for their own children.

108 When I ask Stoney people why alleged injustices by Chiefs are allowed to continue, one of the answers I get is the 'residential school mentality' of many of the people. They say that they were so conditioned to being told what to think that they do not think for themselves and they accept authority without question.

The Criminalization of Religious Practices

109 Throughout the pre-contact centuries the Aboriginal people had survived the difficulties of their existence with the help of spiritual ceremonies. These were declared pagan and criminal. Pipe ceremonies, sundances, sweat lodges and other practices were part of their coping and healing, and when they faced the most disruptive events of their existence, the dominance by a foreign culture, they did not have the benefit of their spiritual ceremonies to help them cope.

"In 1884 and 1885 the potlatch and the sundance, two of the most visible and spiritually significant aspects of coastal and plains culture respectively, were outlawed." (Volume 1 p. 183)

Indian Agents

110   After the treaties were signed the Federal Government appointed Indian Agents to administer them. These men were given almost absolute authority. Indians could not stand for election as chief without the approval of the agent. The agent had the authority to have Indians whipped if he considered it necessary. The agent decided who received food and other necessaries. Indians who were no longer able to support themselves by hunting and gathering, because they were prohibited from leaving the reserve, were reduced to sitting around the agents office waiting for handouts. This led to the unfortunate people who were referred to as Agency Indians.

111   A serious effect that this is having today is that many of the current Aboriginal Chiefs grew up subject to these Indian Agents, and they were the only role model of Government that they knew.

10. Cultural Differences

112   In the Highway case reference was made on behalf of the accused to The Cawsey Report. The court said at page 158:

> "Neither a trial court nor an appellate court is likely to be impressed by some vague reference to cultural differences between Aboriginal communities and non-Aboriginal society unsupported by more."

113   It may not be possible to do anything more than make vague references to cultural differences because they are so hard to understand and even if understood would be equally difficult to articulate. I have set out my rudimentary understanding of some of the cultural factors which I attribute to the reluctance of witnesses in giving testimony, and I will now set out a summary of other differences as I understand them. I have relied on the books Dancing with a Ghost and Returning to the Teachings, by Rupert Ross, for much of my information, and I have had the opportunity to discuss this with him. He has cautioned me against generalizing cultural attributes, as they vary between individual Aboriginals and Aboriginal groups. He has worked mostly with the Ojibwa and Cree of Northern Ontario, and claims no knowledge of the Stoney. My observations and inquiries of the Stoney satisfy me that their culture has much in common with his observations of the Ojibwa and Cree. Ross has also said that short quotes from his carefully built context may make him seem more declarative than he wants to be.

114   With these caveats, I will begin with the following from Dancing with a Ghost.

> "... our two cultures are, in my view, separated by an immense gulf, one which the Euro-Canadian culture has never recognized, much less tried to explore and accommodate.
>
> In retrospect, the discovery of such a gulf should not have been surprising. The fact that it was suggests the assumption that Indians were probably just "primitive versions" of us, a people who needed only to "catch up" to escape the poverty and despair which afflicts far too many of their communities." [p. xxii]

115   I believe that most Euro-Canadians are operating on the "primitive version" assumption and that it is having a very negative effect on their attitude toward these people. The fact that they did not have the written word, gunpowder and other

technology allowed Europeans to disregard all aspects of their lives. My study of their culture satisfies me that there is much the Europeans could have learned from them and that is still so.

116 Many Euro-Canadians seem to feel that with our technology we have given them more than we have taken. I believe that most of them share the sentiment of the Great Sioux Chief and Holy Man Sitting Bull, who said

> The life of white men is slavery. They are prisoners in towns or farms. The life my people want is a life of freedom. I have seen nothing a white man has, houses or railways or clothing or food, that is as good as the right to move in the open country, and live in our own fashion. (James Creelman, On the Great Highway: The Wanderings and Adventures of a Special Correspondent. Boston: Lothrop Publishing Co., 1901, p. 301. Quoted by Robert M. Utley in The Lance and the Shield: The Life and Times of Sitting Bull)

Spirituality

117 I find that Aboriginal people generally are more spiritual than Euro Canadians. They usually start meetings and other functions with a prayer and often with a smudge, a sacred ceremony in which they burn sweet grass.

118 They share a pantheist view of the world. Everything has a spirit, and they respect the spirit in all living, plant and inorganic things. When they killed an animal for food they prayed to the spirit of the animal to ask forgiveness for killing it and to thank it for supplying them with food and other things for which they used it. This belief that all things have a spirit, and that all spirits are somehow connected, seems to have them place a much higher value on abstract things than does the materialism of non-Aboriginal society.

119 I see this as putting many Aboriginals at a disadvantage in the material world of today, because many are not motivated to compete for material things, but then suffer when they are deprived of them.

Worldview

120 The religious belief of Judaeo-Christian Europeans and the Aboriginal belief results in our viewing ourselves at the top of creation, while they view themselves at the bottom.

> "In Judaeo-Christian tradition God created man and ...
> "God said, Let us make man in our image and likeness to rule the fish in the sea, the birds of heaven, the cattle, all wild animals on earth, and all reptiles that crawl upon the earth ..."
>
> It (Aboriginal tradition) places the Mother Earth (and her life blood, the waters) in first place, for without them there would be no plant, animal or human life. The plant world stands second, for without it there would be no animal or human life. The animal is third. Last, and clearly least important within this unique hierarchy, come humans. Nothing whatever depends on our survival." Returning to the Teachings p. 61

121 I suggest that this different belief system results in a virtuous humility in many traditional Aboriginals, and an unfortunate arrogance in many non-Aboriginals, and that these traditionally different attitudes have made the Aboriginal vulnerable to exploitation.

Human Interaction

122 In my dealings with the Stoney people one of the most impressive conversations I have had is with a woman who is a wellness facilitator. Her first husband was killed some years ago by a drunk driver. Her niece was killed by another drunk driver last year. The niece was a beautiful young woman and mother and a rodeo star. I would expect people of my culture to feel nothing but anger, hatred, and a desire for revenge against the man who killed such a person. This woman told me she was very concerned for that man because he was so depressed by what he had done that he was suicidal, and so she was participating in healing circles to try and help him.

123 My first reaction was to think that this woman had a tremendous capacity for forgiveness, but as I have studied the traditional Aboriginal culture I now think that it doesn't even really involve forgiveness, because forgiveness presupposes the concept of punishment, and that is not part of her culture.

124 This phenomenon of accepting people and things the way they are without criticism or complaint and without overt action to change them is something which Rupert Ross deals with in Dancing With a Ghost and he speaks of the "ethic of non-interference," (p. 12) the "ethic that anger not be shown," (p. 28) the "ethic respecting praise and gratitude" (p. 34) and the "conservation-withdrawal tactic" (p. 35).

Human Development

125 In white society our emphasis is on the development of the individual as is demonstrated by the fact that virtually all of our human rights legislation is based on individual freedom. The Aboriginal emphasizes relationship.

126 In The Sacred Tree, a book produced by over thirty elders, spiritual teachers and professionals from across North America, the Twelve Principles of Indian Philosophy begin with WHOLENESS. All things are interrelated. Everything in the

universe is part of a single whole. Everything is connected in some way to everything else. It is only possible to understand something if we understand how it is connected to everything else. (Returning to the Teachings, p. 63)

127 Again I see a virtuous quality working to the disadvantage of these people. While helping others is a universally accepted virtue, the Aboriginal, who believes that 'making it together' should be the rule, is at a great disadvantage in a society where 'making it on your own' is the rule.

Relationship to Nature

128 The thousands of years in which Aboriginals were dependant on nature and their spiritual view that had every animal, plant, and even the rocks possessing their own spirits, resulted in a unique respect for all of nature. This is in stark contrast to the destruction of forests and fish stocks and every other element of nature that is being perpetrated by white society's so called 'developers.'

Social Order

129 In the pre-contact period there were no 'Chiefs' as we think of them today. On a hunt the group would follow the best hunter, in war they would follow the best warrior, in picking berries they would follow the best berry picker, but the concept of someone who had authority over others was foreign to them.

130 Rupert Ross speaks of an Aboriginal woman's view of hierarchies:

> "... the problem was not so much the abuse of power by those who held it. Instead, it was the giving of such power to individuals or small groups in the first place. She told us that her people wanted to get away from "the hierarchies of the whiteman," hierarchies imposed on her people in

every way. ... They wanted to restore the situation" where none received such power over others, where such decisions came out of the clans and families from the bottom up, not the top down." [Returning to the Teachings, p. 55]

Family Construct

131 The Aboriginal people form their families differently from us, and differently from each other. The Stoney are Nakoda Sioux. They form their family relationships according to the Crow kinship system. From the point of view of a child in this system his biological parents are his mother and father, but all of his mother's sisters, and all of his father's brothers are also called mother and father. The mother's brothers and the father's sisters are his aunts and uncles. All the people his parents call mother or father are his grandparents, all of the children of people he calls mother, father, are his brothers and sisters.

132 When the missionaries first encountered Aboriginal society they could not see their European based concept of family in this different construct, and they came to the conclusion that there was no family construct. This must have been at least a part of the justification for taking the children into the residential schools, which were often referred to as 'orphanages.'

View of Human Nature

133 In Dancing With a Ghost, Rupert Ross has a chapter which is entitled 'The Doctrine of Original Sanctity,' in which he compares the Aboriginal view of human nature as basically good to the Judaeo-Christian view of human nature which starts with our fallen nature and original sin.

134 He relates these views to their effect on our responses to criminal activity:

"If it is your conviction the people live one short step from hell, that it is more natural to sin than to do good, then your response as a judicial official will be to use terror to prevent the taking of that last step backward. You will be quick to threaten offenders with dire consequences should they "slide back" into their destructive ways. ... If, by contrast, it is your conviction that people live one step away from heaven, you will be more likely to respond by coaxing them gently forward, by encouraging them to progress, to realize the goodness within them, the use of coercion, threats or punishment by those who would serve as guides to goodness would seem a denial of the very vision that inspires them." (p. 169)

The Role of Women

135 In the traditional Aboriginal society women had a separate but equal role with men. This role was changed by European influence. Because of the male dominated nature of European society, the first explorers and traders would only deal with the men, and when trade became important to the Aboriginal, the role of women declined significantly. This process was furthered by the dominance given to Indian men in the Indian Acts.

11. Alcohol and Violence

"Alcoholism must be treated as a disease and not as a crime. "The Cawsey Report" (p. 8-6)."

136 When one considers the historic, cultural, social and political circumstances of Aboriginal offenders, I suggest it becomes evident that alcohol and violence are the results of injustice which these people have suffered.

"... poverty, loss of culture and tradition, unemployment, inadequate health services, inadequate education and training, family breakdown and racism must be recognized as factors which contribute to criminal activity by Aboriginals." (The Cawsey Report p. 8-2)

There is no doubt in our minds that economic and social deprivation is a major underlying cause of disproportionately high rates of crime among Aboriginal people. (The Royal Commission Justice Report p. 42)

We have concluded that over-representation (in the Criminal Justice system) is linked directly to the particular and distinctive historical and political processes that have made Aboriginal people poor beyond poverty. (The Royal Commission Justice Report p. 46)

137 The tremendous violence that I see all too often in this community is, in my view, a result of social conditions combined with the cultural characteristics of non-interference, non-criticism, and not expressing anger. These cultural restraints seem to result in anger being internalized for a much longer time than is traditional in white society, and the result is that when it is released, usually through the use of alcohol, it is often much more violent.

138 Given all of the above, it is my view that the provisions of the Code require an emphasis on treatment, and that not only justice but morality require that this be emphasized in relation to Aboriginal peoples.

REILLY PROV. CT. J.

cp/s/mii/drs/drs/drs

FURTHER READING

Books

Dickason, Olive P. *Canada's First Nations: A History of Founding Peoples from Earliest Times.* Toronto: McClelland & Stewart, 1992.

Gorman, Ruth, and Frits Pannekoek. *Behind the Man: John Laurie, Ruth Gorman and the Indian Vote in Canada.* University of Calgary Press, 2007.

Reports

Cawsey, Allan. "Report of the Task Force on the Canadian Criminal Justice System and Its Impact on the Indian and Métis People of Alberta," Mar. 1, 1991 (the Cawsey Report). 3 vols. Edmonton: Alberta Ministry of Justice; and Calgary: Alberta Heritage Digitization Project (University of Calgary). Accessed 20100308 in PDF at http://is.gd/a3ArP.

Reilly, Prov. Ct. J. "Report of a Public Inquiry under the Fatality Inquiries Act held at the Provincial Court in Cochrane, Alta., on Feb. 26, 1999 (and by adjournment on Jun. 11, 1999) into the death of Sherman Laron Labelle. Canmore: Provincial Court of Alberta, September 16, 1999.

Royal Commission on Aboriginal Peoples (RCAP). "Report of the Royal Commission on Aboriginal Peoples." 7 vols. Ottawa: Canada Communication Group, 1996. Accessed 20100625 in HTML at http://is.gd/d9lt7.

Royal Commission on Aboriginal Peoples (RCAP). "Choosing Life: Special Report on Suicide among Aboriginal People." Ottawa: Canada Communication Group, 1995.

Cases

R. v. Brady, 1998 ABCA 7 (CanLII) [Alta. C.A.]

R. v. Brown, Highway and Umphreville, 1992 CanLII 2829 [Alta. C.A.]

R. v. Gladue, 1999 CanLII 679 [S.C.C.]

R. v. Hunter (1997), 1998 ABCA 141 (CanLII) [Alta. C.A.]

R. v. McDonnell, 1997 CanLII 389 [S.C.C.]

R. v. Williams, 1998 CanLII 782 [S.C.C.]

Statutes

Criminal Code, R.S.C. 1985, c. C-46, sections 718, 718.1, 718.2

Fatality Inquiries Act, R.S.A. 2000, c. F-9

Provincial Court Act, R.S.A. 2000, c. P-31

The complete texts of all of the cases and statutes mentioned in this work are freely available online from CanLII, the Canadian Legal Information Institute, at www.canlii.org.

Much of the media coverage mentioned in chapter 12 is available in full text from the ProQuest database, online through most public libraries. A user's manual in PDF is at http://is.gd/bSuKA, or ask your local librarian.

INDEX OF NAMES

JUDGE JOHN REILLY was appointed to the bench at age 30 and had the distinction of having been the youngest Provincial Court Judge in Alberta history. At 50 he made a promise to himself that he was going to improve the delivery of justice to the Stoney Nakoda First Nation at Morley. Reilly retired in 2008 but continues to sit as a supernumerary judge.